The Sage Gateshead

The Deutsche Bibliothek
holds a record for this
publication in the Deutsche
Nationalbibliografie; detailed
bibliographical data can be
found under http://dnb.ddb.de

Library of Congress Control
Number: 2009936678

©2010, Foster + Partners,
London, and Prestel Verlag,
Munich · Berlin · London ·
New York

Prestel Verlag, A Member
of Verlagsgruppe Random
House GmbH

Prestel Verlag
Königinstrasse 9
80539 Munich
Germany
Tel +49 (089) 242908-300
Fax +49 (089) 242908-335
www.prestel.de

Prestel Publishing
900 Broadway, Suite 603
New York NY 10003
USA
Tel +1 (212) 995-2720
Fax +1 (212) 995-2733

Prestel Publishing Ltd
4 Bloomsbury Place
London WC1A 2QA
UK
Tel +44 (020) 7323-5004
Fax +44 (020) 7636-8004
www.prestel.com

ISBN 978-3-7913-4314-3

The Sage Gateshead Foster + Partners

Anthony Sargent
Peter Buchanan

PRESTEL
MUNICH · BERLIN · LONDON · NEW YORK

Norman Foster's sketches
explore the arrangement of the
building as a series of orthogonal
auditoria enveloped by a taut
canopy roof. In one sketch he
refers to the clam shell-like forms
of the Sydney Opera House,
in which the exterior profile
is formed independently of the
internal spaces – a strategy
he rejects.

Introduction Anthony Sargent

At the time The Sage Gateshead opened in 2004 the architects were often asked by the media whether they had set out to create a new icon for Tyneside. They replied that their overriding intention had been to create a series of spaces that would prove functionally and aesthetically hospitable to a range of carefully specified uses. In that aim the design team have succeeded brilliantly, but they have also created – whether or not it was their intention – an inspiring new emblem for the ongoing cultural renaissance of Newcastle Gateshead, where over £250 m has been spent in eight years creating five completely new cultural institutions and vividly characterised refurbishments of six more.

Like the Swiss Re building in London, The Sage Gateshead peeps into view from innumerable vantage points on Tyneside, sometimes all of it visible, sometimes partially but unmistakably glimpsed between other buildings – or, teasingly, for seven seconds from the Edinburgh-bound trains as they leave Newcastle. Not unlike the sea fifteen minutes away, the perpetual dancing miracle of the roof with its 3,000 linen-finished steel panels offers an almost infinite juxtaposition of colours and patterns as the changing light falls on them. Like the Angel of the North, the decision not to light the building's roof

externally at night has been triumphantly vindicated, as the evening warmth of the interior lighting radiates out across the river, offering its own enticing welcome to local people and visitors to explore the riches within. Already, long before you reach the doors, the confidence and warmth of The Sage Gateshead's welcome is unmistakable.

The architects spoke eloquently during the design process about their desire to welcome the arriving visitor with an ambitiously omnivorous 'urban room', but nothing promised by the design team prepared us for the daily miracle of The Sage Gateshead's main Concourse and foyers. That wonderful phrase in Peter Buchanan's essay, of the Concourse as a 'social condenser: a great mixing machine where all the building's different functions and their users meet' is precisely how this magnificent space works, sweeping up in its embrace an enormous range of different kinds of visitors and users of The Sage Gateshead.

Our music programme includes almost every imaginable kind of classical and vernacular music, and with that diversity comes an exactly parallel diversity of audiences. In our early days we were careful about the juxtapositions of different kinds of music (and therefore audiences) that we programmed simultaneously. But the combination of the architectural miracle of the Concourse with Geordies' natural inquisitive confidence quickly made that unnecessary. Now, night after night, rock enthusiasts rub shoulders with classical aficionados, the folk community with explorers of world music, and – with a seemingly effortless confidence – the public spaces of The Sage Gateshead encourage a kind of easy-going social mingling which is really very rare in music centres. And it's not only our adult visitors who have taken to the Concourse. Every day with the start of our under-fives classes there is a cheery cavalcade of eager toddlers with their adults in tow and – strikingly – far from being in any way intimidated by the grandeur of the space, they treat it with a natural sense of ownership, often lying on the floor sketching or reading while the adults catch a moment for a coffee if they have arrived early.

Perhaps the architects foresaw that consequence of their design. But one consequence which I think has surprised us all is the way our public spaces lend themselves so very well to festivals. Intricately interlocking schedules of performances in the three halls and on stages on the Concourse, and linked workshops in the Music Education Centre, see our visitors in constant amiably turbulent flows up and down the stairs, in and out of the halls, pausing at the bars or the café to compare notes on what they have just seen and heard.

The Sage Gateshead has proved the quintessential festival building, not just for the audiences we've welcomed but also for artists, who tell us, time after time, how that wonderfully informal immediacy of the public experience enhances their own pleasure in playing here. For our summer festivals we've now completed the complementary outdoor performance space immediately to the east of the building, seating a further 1,000 at chairs and tables on the hard standing and on the grass risers with their unbeatable views across the Tyne to Newcastle.

The halls themselves unfailingly work their own magic on artists and audiences alike. Audiences value, even if unconsciously, the blend of warmth, clarity and impact, which is the acoustic hallmark of all the working spaces in The Sage Gateshead. The technical sophistication of the halls allows for a huge range of theatrical lighting and constant rearrangements of the staging, so people coming back to a hall for a different kind of performance can suppose they are in an entirely different space. Artists tell us how much they value the subtle design approach that gives them an unusually immediate sense of contact with their audiences. Over the first five years of The Sage

Gateshead, 2,500 performances have covered the musical spectrum. Increasingly we find the halls are as suitable for staged and multi-media events as they are for concerts.

Meanwhile the twenty-six teaching, practice and rehearsal rooms of the Music Education Centre have achieved another small but important miracle of their own. Soon after The Sage Gateshead opened, students known to hate the discipline of practice started telling us they looked forward to coming to practise here, partly enjoying the building's overall ambience but also finding the acoustics and the simple elegance of the Music Education Centre rooms an encouragement to practise of a kind they had never encountered before.

Furthermore, although the idea of conferencing was described to the design team simply in terms of income generation, they also ensured that the rooms offer the same stylish, sensitive ambience to conference delegates as to music visitors. The fact that The Sage Gateshead now earns from conferencing more than three times the sum originally projected has a lot to do with how much conference organisers enjoy the experience of bringing their conventions, meetings and functions to this unique waterfront location.

Ever since The Sage Gateshead was conceived, we envisaged it as a working environment, where rehearsal and practice would be visible, artists would be encouraged to stretch themselves beyond their comfort zones, audiences would feel inspired to explore new kinds of music, and students would feel their own labours in perfect consonance with the general working flavour of the building. The architects embraced that unusual kind of vision fastidiously. Countless tiny elements of detailing encourage that sense of joyful purpose in almost everyone who comes to The Sage Gateshead – even if their purpose is simply to extract every ounce of pleasure from hearing an artist they have long admired perform in one of the world's finest and most sympathetic concert rooms. The huge window allowing visitors to watch musicians at work in the Northern Rock Foundation Hall; the almost always-open Viewing Box allowing visitors to sit in on all rehearsals (and technical preparation) in Hall One; the way visitors can stroll through the Music Education Centre (not into the teaching rooms of course, but watching through the windows); everything about the experience of visiting or using The Sage Gateshead confirms our wish to make its core purposes immediately legible.

Throughout our first five years the international media have showered praise on The Sage Gateshead – both as a piece of architecture and as a platform for world class music-making – but in our own experience, living and working in The Sage Gateshead, the design team achieved even more than those obvious successes. This is a building which in a quite extraordinary way itself already feels alive. It welcomes its visitors, students, teachers, musicians, administrative staff, security team and housekeepers every day with an almost palpable physical warmth, while at the same time respectfully never overstepping the boundaries of good manners. It treats the audience for Bach's grave B Minor Mass with proper solemnity, while encouraging the audience for young Cuban bands to appropriately Latin extremes of enthusiasm. Its acoustic and functional quality allows the delegates to major conferences to concentrate with unusual focus on the task at hand; to our community of adults with learning difficulties and our youngest toddlers alike it extends a protecting hand. Peter Buchanan's perceptive essay refers to the tight economic envelope within which The Sage Gateshead was conceived, designed and built. However, like all the best designers, the architects have treated that entirely normal real-world constraint not as an impediment but as an inspiration.

As I said at the outset, the architects were at pains to talk carefully about fulfilling the brief rather than generating an icon; but, as so often, by aiming at one target, they hit both. They have created a supremely efficient working machine, and public spaces of real elegance and warmth. But they have also provided a confident new image that represents the spirit of cultural reinvention that has gripped Tyneside for the last decade. Alongside the Tyne Bridge, the Angel of the North and the Gateshead Millennium Bridge, The Sage Gateshead has taken its own defining place in the extraordinary twenty-first century journey of Newcastle Gateshead – in the hearts of the local community and in the eyes of the wider world.

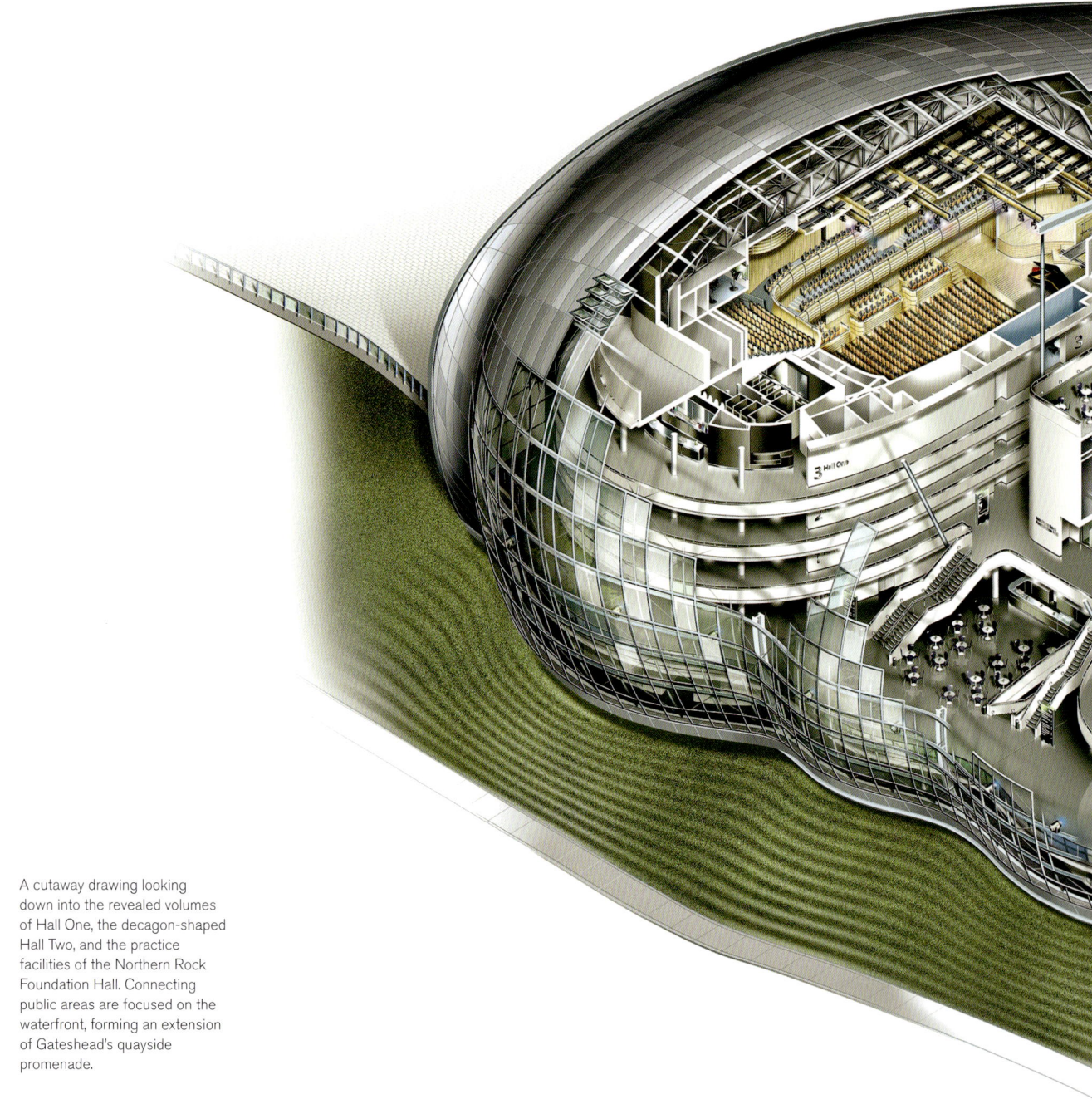

A cutaway drawing looking down into the revealed volumes of Hall One, the decagon-shaped Hall Two, and the practice facilities of the Northern Rock Foundation Hall. Connecting public areas are focused on the waterfront, forming an extension of Gateshead's quayside promenade.

The urban room *par excellence* Peter Buchanan

Looking east from the rail bridge linking Gateshead and Newcastle reveals one of Britain's most memorable views. Glistening at the bottom of the steep sided valley is the Tyne flowing to the sea. High above it is the mighty arch of the Tyne Bridge, and below that the flatter arch of the low-level Swing Bridge. Beyond both is the slender arc of the Gateshead Millennium Bridge supporting a deck that curves in plan and so becomes yet one more arched form when it tilts to let boats pass. Harmonising with all these arches to create a symphony of curves is the swelling silvery form of The Sage Gateshead, in whose stainless-steel roof panels the ever-changing moods of the sky are reflected more vividly than in the waters of the Tyne below.

The visual rapport between the undulating roof and its larger setting is formally resonant and structurally apt. The Sage Gateshead is to an exceptional degree a building designed from the inside out and the outside in – the result of a clear conceptual stance that has been iteratively worked and adjusted to achieve a perfect fit.

Seen from inside, the roof wraps tightly over the two halls, the rehearsal room between them, and the foyer or Concourse along the waterfront. Spaced apart, side by side, the halls are aligned perpendicular to the steep slope, bringing several advantages beyond acoustic separation. Backstage servicing is clearly organised and efficient, with stages, loading docks and connecting routes all at the same level. Set a level below is the elongated Concourse, and tucked into the slope below that is the Music Education Centre. The lucidity of this diagrammatic organisation gives no sense of the immensely rich interactions it spawns, between various kinds of music and between musicians, audience members and people who come to study music at all ages and levels of proficiency.

The Sage Gateshead is Foster + Partners' first building for the performing arts. It is also one of the most programmatically complex buildings the practice has addressed, not only in the range of and contrasts between the functions housed but also in the many cross-fertilising interactions between both these functions and the people involved in them. The result is what could be seen as a most un-Foster-like building, one quite lacking the typical consistency of architectural language where, say, interiors are to some degree predictable from a reading of the outside and spaces are fitted out and furnished from a highly selective palette. Instead, the enveloping steel roof is in quite a different idiom to the smoothly

Right: An aerial image of the site. The original intention was to position the building close to the Baltic Flour Mills. Ultimately it was moved further west, to allow the Baltic and The Sage Gateshead to frame the regenerated Gateshead riverside.

plastered white 'exteriors' of the three halls within; and these in turn give no sense of their interiors, each richly modulated in wood, which are again very different from one another. The degree to which these spaces, though highly flexible, are tightly tailored, is also atypical of Foster, who usually achieves flexibility through a looser-fit accommodation of function.

Yet the dominant space in the building, even if unlike anything Foster had built to date, is one of the best examples of a device Foster and his colleagues have developed through a series of projects to become a key feature of some of the practice's buildings. The Concourse foyer is what has been called an 'urban room', which here fully lives up to Foster's claim that it is an 'urban living room'. The urban room is an internal extension of the public realm where members of the public can take possession of the building and meet as equals those who are more involved with the building and its various activities, in this case musicians, music teachers and students.

As here, Foster's urban rooms are central to the function and life of the buildings, embodying their essential spirit and identity. But even as urban rooms go, this one is remarkable for the range of activities and interactions to which it is host. Also, while some urban rooms – such as the Great Court at the British

Museum – are embedded as the 'heart' of the building, others establish intensified visual connections with the city outside, as does this Concourse with its splendid views of the Tyne and the Newcastle waterfront. The other major element of The Sage Gateshead that belongs to a lengthening and ever evolving strand in Foster's architecture is the enveloping roof, yet one more exploration of complex double-curved geometric topologies. However, in contrast to the work of many other architects exploring such topologies, this is no wilful 'blob' but the disciplined product of the quest for economy and efficiency.

Relatively well-to-do Newcastle-upon-Tyne – birthplace of the steam engine and electric light, and now more famous for its nightlife and cultural ambitions – and the less affluent Gateshead were once independent industrial centres respectively on the north and south banks of the Tyne. Though they retain separate municipal administrations they are otherwise now fusing into the single conurbation of Newcastle Gateshead. Together, they and the larger hinterland of North-East England had long lacked a home for the regional orchestra, Northern Sinfonia, as well as a concert venue for visiting orchestras and chamber groups, and for folk music and jazz, which have a large following here. Over the years various

Left: A concept sketch by Norman Foster exploring the positioning of the building and the way in which the Concourse could facilitate circulation patterns parallel to the river and open up views across the Tyne.

sites in Newcastle had been mooted for a concert hall complex. Then Gateshead Council, alert to the powerful role that culture can play as a spur to urban regeneration, seized the opportunity to consolidate what it had begun with the conversion of a riverside flourmill into the Baltic Centre for Contemporary Art, and offered a large adjacent site for a new music centre.

In 1997 architects were invited to submit three panels outlining how they might approach the project and from this large group six international firms were asked to present more detailed proposals. The Foster team, led by Spencer de Grey, Robin Partington and Jason Flanagan, won the commission. Having done so, their first move was to start afresh, recognising that a properly developed and detailed brief needed to be elaborated with input from representatives of all the different user groups, as well as from crucial consultants such as acousticians and stage design specialists. The Foster team also proposed moving the building upstream and upslope slightly, but still within the parcel of land owned by Gateshead Council.

The Sage Gateshead now sits on a site where coal was once loaded on to ships docked below. Behind it is a run of brick arches, dating from the site's industrial past, and in front of it is a Royal Navy facility

on the river's edge. The building's siting has the effect of spreading rather than concentrating the impact of the Baltic and The Sage Gateshead, these two cultural facilities thus becoming the 'magnetic attractor poles' of what will be a mixed-use development on the Gateshead banks of the Tyne. More than that, an active loop of urban attractions has been created that makes the most of the larger setting on both sides of the river. From the Newcastle Quayside – with its bars and restaurants – there is a natural route that crosses the Gateshead Millennium Bridge, takes in the adjacent Baltic, then climbs up to and cuts through The Sage Gateshead, before descending to the Swing Bridge and reconnecting with the Newcastle waterfront.

Spencer de Grey notes that Gateshead Council was an inspirational client: 'Starting with the Angel of the North, followed by the new bridge, then the Baltic Arts Centre, and finally The Sage Gateshead, they have promoted a strong programme of urban regeneration through the arts.' Central to the success of any cultural building is the early involvement of the end user. The North Music Trust was already in place with representatives of Northern Sinfonia, Folkworks and Northern Arts able to play a key role in the development of the design. This was an unusually

Right: An early sketch model, in which nylon stocking material was stretched over framing to study the form of the roof.

broad-based client body, which explains much about the spirit that informs the design and running of the building. Early on, the client appointed Arup Acoustics as acousticians and Theatre Projects to advise on the design of the halls and their stages. Together with the architects, these consultants toured concert halls in the UK and mainland Europe, to learn first-hand from precedent and get a better idea of the kinds of hall that would work best here, a process that also helped bond them as a team. Later, other consultants, including structural and environmental engineers and cost consultants, would contribute to the evolving design.

From the investigation of what best suited each group in the client body and the study of other music centres it became clear that two halls were required. One would be a full-sized concert hall, for the resident Northern Sinfonia, visiting orchestras and other large-scale groups of all musical genres; the other a smaller, more intimate hall for chamber music, folk, jazz and other sorts of performance. Both halls were thus to be as flexible as possible. There would also be a rehearsal room, large enough to accommodate a full orchestra, which could be used for performances and various other functions too and would be the focal point of the music school. Despite the tight budget, there would be no skimping on the halls. Ensuring their quality was a priority so as to attract the best performers, meet the exacting expectations of today's concert-goers, and be flexible enough to earn extra revenue from conferences and recording sessions. The halls would take their ideal shape as independent volumes separated from each other under the umbrella-like embrace of an independent roof. Savings, especially on finishes, would be made elsewhere.

Education and community participation would also be priorities. Education would take many forms, not only those based in the Music Education Centre, which teaches those intending a career in music and provides chances for everybody to participate in music-making. There would be an ambitious region-wide participatory programme as well, based at The Sage Gateshead but active throughout the North of England. Like any cultural pursuit, concert going is itself educational and the programming of concerts with a wide mix of genres was to encourage exploration and a broad engagement with music.

Education also involves informal meeting with, and learning from, others. To this end, the Concourse would be almost a machine for provoking mixing, meeting and participation, where the interactions

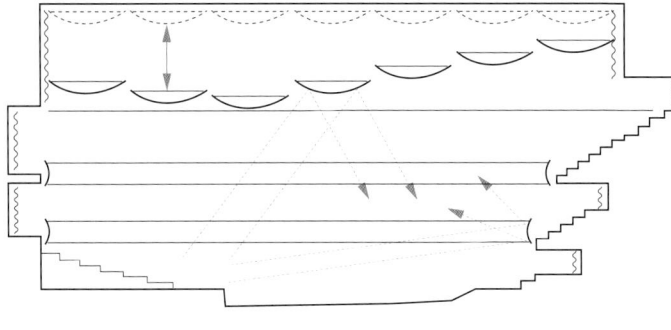

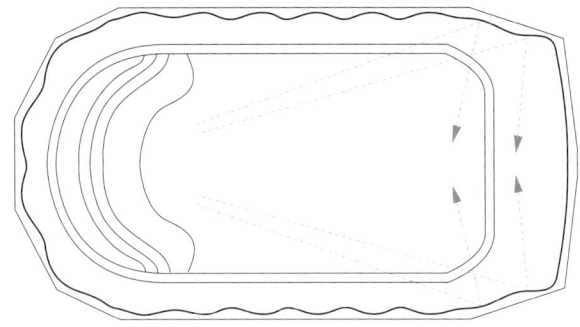

with all kinds of different groups would encourage a sense of involvement and even of ownership of the building and its activities.

Once the potential of the Concourse to become an urban room, which mediated between the building and the city and between the concert halls and the education centre, had been grasped, the basic organisation of the design began to fall into place. A through route on the larger urban loop, the Concourse would be an internalised, multi-functional part of the public realm enlivened by the various activities along, above and below it. From here it was a short step to realising also the consequent advantage in the servicing of the halls, and that the separate elements of the interior could all be enveloped under a tent-like roof that would unify them despite their relative formal independence.

Nevertheless, once this schematic arrangement had been settled on, much work still had to go into refining each part of the building, especially the halls. These had to meet very exacting standards, ensuring a total absence of background noise and delivering a sound of great strength and impact that combines clarity of individual notes with a richness of blend to the total sound. The position of some elements changed too: the larger hall, which has come to be

Left: A sectional model of the 1,700-seat Hall One, with diagrams illustrating the principle of the reflecting surfaces in both section and plan. The first wave of sound is directly from the orchestra; secondary sounds are reflected from the walls and balconies; tertiary sound reflection comes from the ceiling. Movable panels allow the room height to be adjusted between 10 and 21 metres to suit a wide variety of music types.

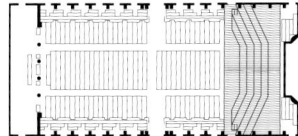 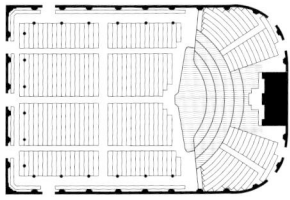

called Hall One, had been centrally placed; but this was deemed to give it undue prominence. It was therefore moved to one side to 'balance' the smaller Hall Two, with the rehearsal room (the Northern Rock Foundation Hall) forming a central pivot.

Hall One is a classic shoebox modelled on such nineteenth-century precedents as the Musikverein in Vienna, which is renowned for its acoustics. Relatively long and narrow, the Musikverein is 48 metres long, 19 metres wide and 18 metres high, with seating for 1,740 and standing room for 300. Its size, shape and capacity are considered ideal for the warm resonant acoustic best suited for symphonic music of the Romantic period. With a little adjustment it is also perfect for the smaller orchestras of the Baroque and Classical eras, and for chamber music. Hall One is of a similar size: 45 metres long, 24 metres wide and 21 metres high, and seats 1,700.

A thoroughly tried-and-tested type, the shoebox is now so well understood acoustically that its design requires less of the complex computer modelling, and none of the testing of large-scale physical models, required when designing halls of other configurations. Indeed, Arup Acoustics has a computer program that can replicate the listening experience of several famous shoebox halls, from any seat you choose.

This same program also predicts the listening experience of halls under design. Another major advantage of the shoebox is that it lends itself, again using tried-and-tested devices such as movable ceiling panels and acoustically absorbent curtains, to easy adjustment for any other type of music, including amplified music, and speech. (A significant daytime source of revenue for such halls is hosting conferences.)

Typical of the shoebox form, the stage of Hall One is at one end of gently raked stalls, which in this instance are overlooked by slightly raised banks of seats along the sides and at the rear. Above these are two shallow galleries that continue behind the stage – so that the audience encircles the players as equal participants in the concert – and extend into deeper balconies at the back of the hall. The basic rectilinearity of the type is softened by rounding the back of the stage, tapering the balconies and rounding most other corners, as well as, in the vertical plane, the fronts of the galleries. The curve of the gallery fronts, and the horizontal slots in the facing panels, serve to diffuse particular sound frequencies. Other curved elements range in scale from the shallower curves of the suspended ceiling panels to the ripples made up of multiple timber battens projecting by

Above left: The form of Hall One is influenced by the 'shoebox' form of Vienna's nineteenth-century Grosser Musikvereinsaal, widely considered to be the best of its kind. Its superior acoustics are due in part to the rectangular shape, the highly modelled wall surfaces and its relatively small volume.

Above right: Another important reference was the Amsterdam Concertgebouw. The hall is also rectangular, though wider than the Vienna hall and a fifth of the audience is seated on stadium steps behind the orchestra. Its decorative plaster wall surfaces and coffered ceiling produce excellent sound diffusion.

Below left: An early sectional model of the 450-seat Hall Two. Developed around consultant Iain Mackintosh's idea of a flexible courtyard theatre, the hall provides a home for Folkworks, Britain's leading folk music organisation.

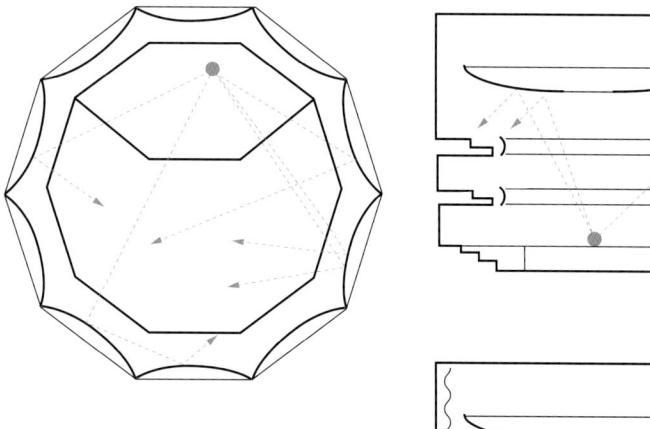

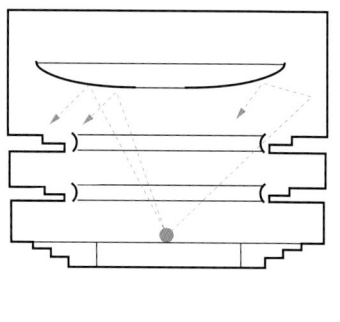

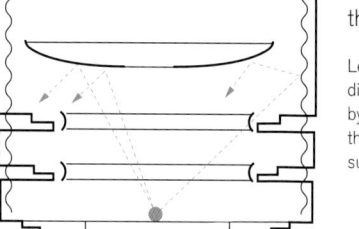

Left: Plan and section acoustic diagrams of Hall Two, produced by Arup Acoustics to illustrate the principle of the reflecting surfaces.

differing amounts along the side walls. All perform an acoustic function. It is the diversity and different scales of these elements that in part determines the overall richness of sound of the hall. All these sound diffusing elements are made of or faced in wood, a blond ash that together with the richly coloured upholstery of the seating gives the room a wonderful golden visual warmth.

Many people are under the misapprehension that the use of wood also gives warmth to the sound of a hall, in a manner analogous to the resonating body of a stringed instrument. But in fact warmth and clarity of sound in an auditorium requires reflecting surfaces of extreme rigidity, particularly to avoid the absorption of low frequency sounds. Here, for instance on the side walls, that is achieved by gluing the wooden battens either directly to the masonry walls or to heavy fibreboard panels that are bolted to the structural walls through an intermediary layer of impregnated felt.

The walls of all three halls are of dense concrete block infilling a structural frame, rather than entirely of poured concrete. For acoustic isolation, and to allow for differential settlement, the structural box of the auditorium, like that of the smaller hall and the rehearsal room, is independent of the rest of the building. It has its own piled foundations, which are sunk 25 metres into a bed of dense clay. Although railway lines run quite close by, the halls are not isolated from these foundations with devices such as rubber dampers, because while the vibration may be detectable to sensitive technical instruments it will always be inaudible to the human ear. The halls are also capped by heavy concrete slabs supported on steel trusses so as to exclude sound from above, including that from the Concourse reflected by the underside of the roof.

Ancillary accommodation wrapped around Hall One provides further acoustic isolation. Behind the stage are the dressing rooms and along each side of the hall are rooms for private entertainment, which also provide the depth for sound-excluding lobbies with double sets of doors to each entrance to the hall. These entrances open off wide galleries that surround the hall from the front of the stage onwards and serve as foyers giving access to its various levels. At the prow of each gallery, where it widens to form a bulge, there is a bar.

Stairs on either side of the hall climb straight up to the galleries from the Concourse. The balustrades edging the stairs and galleries are not of glass, which would be typical of Foster, but are instead solid – and

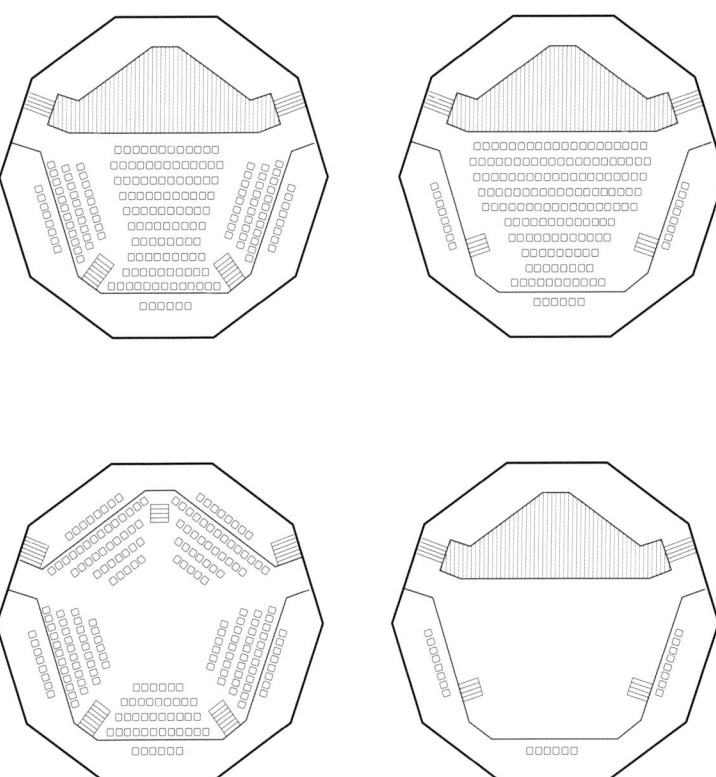

Below: In this early site model
the overall form of the building
is established but the detail
of the external shell has yet
to be resolved.

plastered and painted white, like the outer volumes of the halls. This is not only an economy measure but also provides a comforting sense of containment to the galleries, as well as giving them greater visual presence within the volume of the Concourse and when viewed from outside at night.

Acoustic isolation also required that the halls and rehearsal room be air-conditioned, the only parts of the building that are. (The aerodynamic form of the roof helps to ventilate the rest of the building naturally by channelling the predominant south-westerly wind through the Concourse, while the north-facing glazing on the waterfront admits little solar gain, and the glazed side elevations are shaded by deep porches.) The plant rooms are structurally independent and located behind the building, where they are easily serviced, and the air is distributed through large acoustically insulated ducts to a plenum extending under the stalls.

Fresh air enters the hall through the pedestal of each seat at 0.5 metres a second, the lowest feasible airflow, and then rises through convection to be extracted at the ceiling. As is fairly standard practice, the seats were designed not only for comfort and aesthetics but also for their acoustic performance so that the backs and undersides act as acoustic reflectors while the acoustic of the hall is unaffected by the size of the audience.

The flexibility of Hall One is achieved through a number of devices. Its volume and height can be adjusted by raising and lowering six acoustically reflective ceiling panels, each weighing 14 tonnes. These can be positioned at heights between 10 and 21 metres above the floor of the stalls, to adjust the volume of the hall and the pattern of sound reflections. They can also be positioned to allow musicians to hear themselves better, or spaced so that – though the reflective surface of the ceiling is relatively low – much of the sound passes between the panels and through the slots in them, the reverberation of the full volume of the hall still enriching the sound.

To this end, the volume and hard reflective sides of the hall extend upwards beyond the highest reach of the ceiling panels. For amplified speech and music a much drier acoustic is achieved by drawing out motorised sound-absorbent curtains that can cover as much as 90 per cent of the wall surface. Other than these curtains, and the upholstered seats, there are no sound absorbent surfaces in the hall, in which every shape and detail is designed to support and give strength to the sound.

Right: This simple drawing illustrates how the three-ribbed form of the building's undulating roof was developed as a direct response to the three music halls that it encloses.

The stage was conceived of as a large piece of movable and adjustable furniture, with a basic platform that can be rolled forwards and backwards, and has a slight acoustic resonance to both help project the sound and ensure that the musicians can 'feel' each other's playing. The stage can be customised to suit the size of the orchestra or group by adding or subtracting smaller platforms of various sizes and shapes so that the musicians can see each other as well as be seen by the audience, thus intensifying the sense of integration and participation. When not in use, these platforms are stored behind the stage. Above this store is a loft – part of the acoustic volume of the hall – which anticipates the installation of an organ. For opera and musicals, an orchestra pit can be opened up. The floor of this pit can also be raised to become a 'mosh' pit where members of the audience can dance without obstructing sight-lines during pop and world music concerts, when part of the floor at the rear of the stalls can also be removed to accommodate a sound desk that again does not obstruct sight-lines.

As with the smaller hall and the rehearsal room, no architect seeing photographs of this hall immediately after completion would have guessed it to be by Foster. Closely derived from precedent, warm and

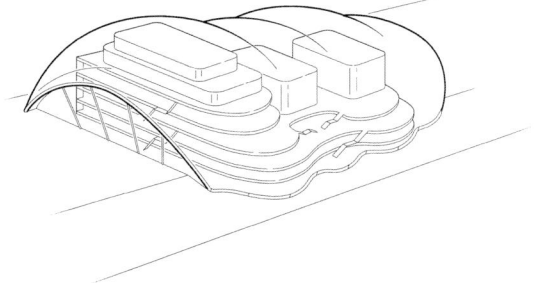

Above and right: Two images of a 1:100 scale model of the building shown with and without the roof. It illustrates the two-part structure of the building's form, as independent auditoria, on the left, and enveloping canopy, on the right.

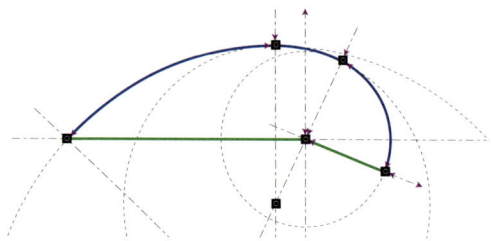
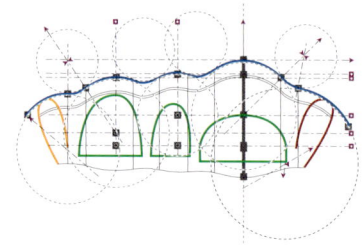

intimate in feeling, and lined entirely in rippling wood to what might seem richly decorative effect, this is the antithesis of what is commonly expected from the Foster studio. Yet it is also a supremely 'functionalist' and high-performance room: every form, material and detail serves a precise purpose, beyond that of also giving the room its very apt character. Just as impressive is how quickly and easily all the changes that give it such adaptability can be accomplished with relatively few staff. Besides functioning brilliantly and having superb acoustics, people like the look and character of the hall so that it is already much loved by audiences and musicians. Perhaps the hall, and indeed the whole building, should be seen as not so much atypical of Foster but rather as proof that the architect is not as easily characterised as some might think, and that the approach of his practice continues to evolve and broaden.

The 400-seat Hall Two is very different in character from Hall One and owes more to theatre than concert hall precedent. It somewhat resembles a miniaturised Elizabethan theatre as well as modern auditoria such as the Crucible Theatre in Sheffield. It is a tall ten-sided prism in volume, intensely intimate and, with its red-stained wood, rather dark and

shadowy, with the atmosphere of a jazz club or pub-theatre. (If such things were not now forbidden, it is easy to imagine it smoke filled and boozy.) Like Hall One it is surrounded by two shallow galleries, but has a flat floor with retractable bleacher seating. In contrast to the galleries this main level is configured as a pentagon, which can be arranged in various ways, such as with a stage on one side or in the centre.

Despite the difference in character and colour, many details are similar to and serve the same purposes as those in Hall One, with a range of curves of various radii diffusing sounds of differing wavelength and motorised curtains used to deaden the acoustic when required. Here, too, the walls continue far above the uppermost gallery to get the requisite volume and area of reflective surface to achieve the desired sound. But there is no plenum under the flat floor: instead fresh conditioned air is let in between the bleacher seats from under the surrounding ambulatory to again rise by stack effect. Air is extracted through grilles at the back of the galleries.

Surrounding the hall to improve acoustic isolation are the enclosed stairs and corridors leading up to the galleries from the single foyer-gallery, which again has a bar at its prow. Like the larger hall, Hall Two is

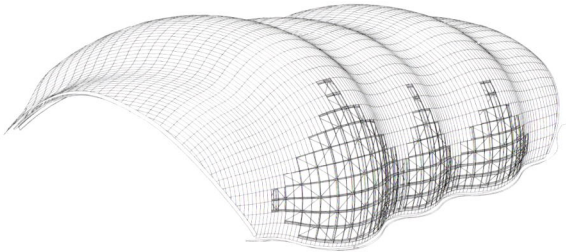

Left: A computer-generated drawing identifying each of the 3,000 stainless-steel roof panels and the 280 double-glazed cladding panels. All the panels are flat.

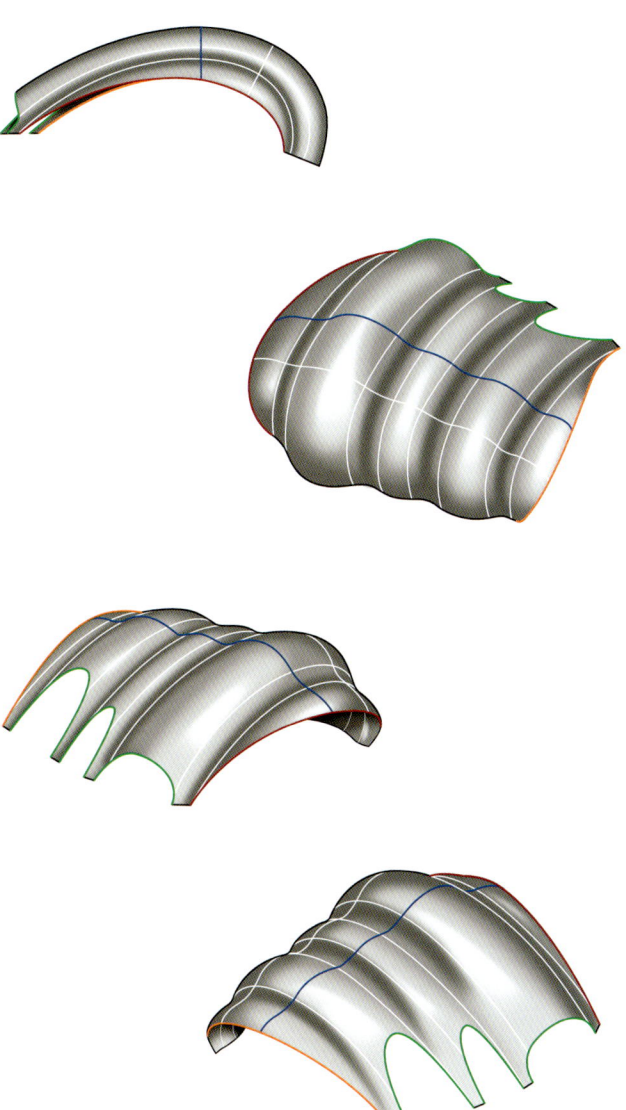

proving very flexible and popular. It is used for a wide range of folk and world music, jazz, contemporary dance, opera, theatre-in-the-round, and chamber music, such as string quartets. With its exceptional acoustics, it is also frequently used for outside broadcast recordings.

The rehearsal room – the Northern Rock Foundation Hall – sits between and is set slightly back from the two halls. Although the lobbies to its twin entrances round off the corners of its 'exterior' volume, it is a rectangular space with shoebox proportions; and though much smaller than Hall One it has been designed with a similar natural acoustic so that musicians adapt easily to the larger hall after rehearsals. Again the acoustic is modulated with wooden battens creating ripples of varying scale to break up and reflect different sound frequencies, while anything up to the whole wall surface can be covered by sound absorbent curtains should the conductor want to deaden the acoustic for analytical purposes, or should it be used for speech or amplified music.

With its flat floor it can accommodate a seated audience of between 200 and 300, depending on how much is set aside for the performers, or be used for other functions such as dances and ceilidhs, banquets and exhibitions. A big window overlooking

Above: This construction photograph shows the steel framing of the roof canopy coming together to form a taut enclosure over the three principal interior volumes.

the Concourse lets musicians see out and people see in; and if the doors are left open, allows rehearsals to be semi-public – a rare pleasure in the music world and one which visitors are quick to say how much they value, in the same way that they appreciate the public viewing box in Hall One.

Behind the rehearsal room is the loading bay that opens directly on to a broad cross-axial route. Besides giving access to the rehearsal room, this leads in one direction almost immediately to the stage of Hall One, and in the opposite direction to the stage of Hall Two. Thus props and big instruments such as grand pianos are easily delivered to any hall, or moved between them. A goods lift on one side of the loading bay allows deliveries to and from the kitchen that serves the brasserie and café on the Concourse level. Behind the cross-axial route, which terminates at its western extreme in the green room (where musicians and performers spend time when not on stage), are the dressing rooms.

Other than these, there are few backstage facilities. This is calculated to ensure that musicians and performers mingle with the public at the bars on the galleries and the café in the Concourse – which the public enjoy, adding to their sense of The Sage Gateshead as a working building.

Above the dressing rooms and the loading bay are the plant rooms for the air-conditioning machinery, while behind Hall Two is a large hospitality room for receptions and dinners, above which are the administrative offices. Complementing the original offices, accommodation has now been added above the rehearsal room beneath the roof, further animating the upper volume of the Concourse.

The Music Education Centre is tucked under the Concourse, against the foundation walls of the halls above, with the practice rooms filling space between these walls and curves that match the edges of the galleries above. The result is a series of twenty-six non-rectangular rooms, the acoustically preferred shape for practice rooms, which are also acoustically isolated, forming boxes of floating timber construction on neoprene pads so as to be independent of structural walls and slabs. In the space between the two crescents of practice rooms is a recording studio. Access to this and the practice rooms is by the serpentine Concourse, which has panoramic views out through the curving glass wall. For the safety of their occupants, all practice rooms also have viewing panels to allow scrutiny from this Concourse. And if the doors are open, the music wafts up into the Concourse, adding yet another dimension to its attractions.

Above: These two images chart the completion of the roof framing and the installation of the roof cladding. The last roof panel was secured in place in April 2004.

The education centre is a crucial part of the building, essential to its very spirit and conception. The range and number of courses and tuition offered here and in the very ambitious and active participation programmes is impressive, varying from a BMus Hons degree undertaken in collaboration with the University of Sunderland to workshops and music appreciation groups for everybody from under-fives to pensioners. Up to 400 people are involved in the local, regional and national teaching programmes run here and from here, the majority of which take place beyond The Sage Gateshead, and from which some one-and-a-half million people benefit. Within the building, members of Northern Sinfonia and folk and other musicians coach individuals and ensembles, and the very active adult education programmes sometimes make use of the rehearsal room and main halls.

In the early stages of design, for economic reasons, a fabric outer roof was considered, pulled down tight over the halls and Concourse as if 'shrink wrapped' to minimise the internal volume and, so again, the cost. Structurally independent of the rest of the building, it was to be designed in collaboration with Buro Happold, a structural engineer with much experience of such roofs. Although it was eventually decided to use a more permanent steel roof, with

better thermal and sound insulation, its form (including the curved 'bites' out of the back) owes something to these origins. The primary structural members are four parallel and unevenly spaced, propped tubular arches spanning front to back, one in each of the gaps between the halls and one at either end of the building. The tall props descend to their footings in the wells alongside the stairs linking the Concourse and balconies or, in one instance, through a slot in the slab above the green room. The asymmetrical shape of the arches is defined as the radii of three circles that decline in radius towards the front of the building so that the curvature of the river frontage is much tighter than at the point where the roof slopes down to the rear service yard.

Spanning across these arches are the wavy purlins that swoop up over each hall to dip down again to the next arch. On top of the purlins is a ribbed steel deck, left exposed as a ceiling. Above that is a layer of thermal and acoustic insulation and then a waterproof membrane. The linen-finished stainless-steel panels on top of this membrane are only a rain-screen, and they sit on rails propped above the waterproof membrane by tubular-steel 'stools' fixed to the purlins.

The roof extends beyond the two outer arches and the side elevations, so forming sheltering porches

Above and above left: Dramatic
lighting and daring acrobatic
performances in the Concourse
formed part of the building's
opening celebrations during
the weekend of 17 – 19
December 2004.

above the entrances to the Concourse and shading the two expansive areas of glazing. On the river-facing north side, the opaque roof also gives way to glazing set flush with the steel panels of the rain-screen. Finalising the pattern of this glazing was one of the last things to be resolved during the design process, after trying a number of alternatives. As completed it takes the form of three stepped pyramids centred on, and reaching up each forward bulge of the roof, to an apex of glass louvres that ventilate the Concourse. These pyramids overlap at their bases so as to give continuous outlook to the Concourse and education levels and reach high enough to give views out from the uppermost balcony.

The Concourse runs the full width of the building, looking out across the river. Open to the public fourteen hours a day, seven days a week, it is the building's main space and urban room, or, to evoke a different period of participatory ideals (the Russian Constructivists of the early Soviet era) its 'social condenser': a great mixing machine where all the building's different functions and their users meet. Also visible together here are some of the differing design idioms of the building's major components. Especially noticeable are the contrasts between the major curved elements of the roof, with its state-of-

the-art computer-derived forms, and with all its structural elements and materials unabashedly revealed, and the white plastered streamlined forms of the halls. The latter also suggest the superstructure of liners and so seem suited to this riverside site as evocations of the ships that once docked below. Curiously, although it is the dominant space of the building, the Concourse could also be described as merely a residual space, what is left over under the sloping roof and in front of and between the forward thrusting halls and balconies.

Conceptually this might be true. Yet a measure of the triumphant synthesis achieved by the design is that the space is shaped precisely to purpose. The bulges of the galleries and those echoing them in the glazing, push and pulsate the space into movement, encouraging visitors to move forward and through the space, passing the information and ticket office counters on the way and pausing where the spatial movement slows to swell into the piazza-like cafeteria. Invitingly noticeable off this space are the elongated spaces extending back into the building, which are occupied by the brasserie, a library and a dedicated space for children.

Animated by the spatial momentum invested by the bulges in the horizontal plane and the soaring

Above and right: Music and music-making is celebrated in all its various forms. Alongside the set-piece performances in the halls are the activities of the Music Education Centre and ad-hoc performances in the Concourse.

curves of the roof that swoop up and out of sight, and enhanced by the spectacular views of the Tyne and internal vistas from its multiple levels, the Concourse is a visually exciting space. It is especially so when packed with people before and after concerts or when used for performances or the display of large-scale art works and installations. The play of projected patterns and images on the white surfaces of the halls adds yet another dimension. Yet the Concourse changes in mood throughout the day, depending on how busy it is, and is equally satisfying when sparsely populated, when the generous scale, the vistas and view, and even the spatial movement, all seem conducive to a more contemplative mood. It is, for instance, the best place in Newcastle Gateshead in which to enjoy a quiet coffee or a drink in the café as the dusk encroaches and then turns to night and the lights of Newcastle form a magical backdrop along one side. It is the urban living room par excellence.

As the Concourse shows in microcosm, what is remarkable about The Sage Gateshead is how many separate elements are brought together and integrated without compromise to the distinctiveness of each. At night, especially, views in through the glazing and the prominence of the bright-lit edges

of the foyer balconies, busy with people, help to establish a sense of scale and human inhabitation.

The Sage Gateshead is clearly hugely successful, an uplifting and lively place that performs all its functions extremely well, including that of encouraging interaction between different groups and the intended sense of participation this brings. It is little wonder that it has been taken warmly to heart by the people of Newcastle Gateshead. Judged as a creative act of public service, it must surely be deemed as among Foster's best works. Its success, as a design and in operation, is a tribute to several contributing factors: the inspired and inclusive vision that informed the brief, and after that, the design and running of the building; the diligent design efforts of a range of specialist skills synthesised by the architectural team; and the proactive, lively and imaginative way all the activities both within and beyond the building are conceived of, coordinated and managed.

The arts have the power to inspire, but they can also help to revitalise a city. The Sage Gateshead is not only a place where people can enjoy a wide range of music, it has been a catalyst for the cultural reinvigoration of Tyneside. Norman Foster, in conversation with the editor, 2009

Above: The form of The Sage Gateshead is echoed by two other Tyneside landmarks: the great arch of the Tyne Bridge and Wilkinson Eyre's Gateshead Millennium Bridge.

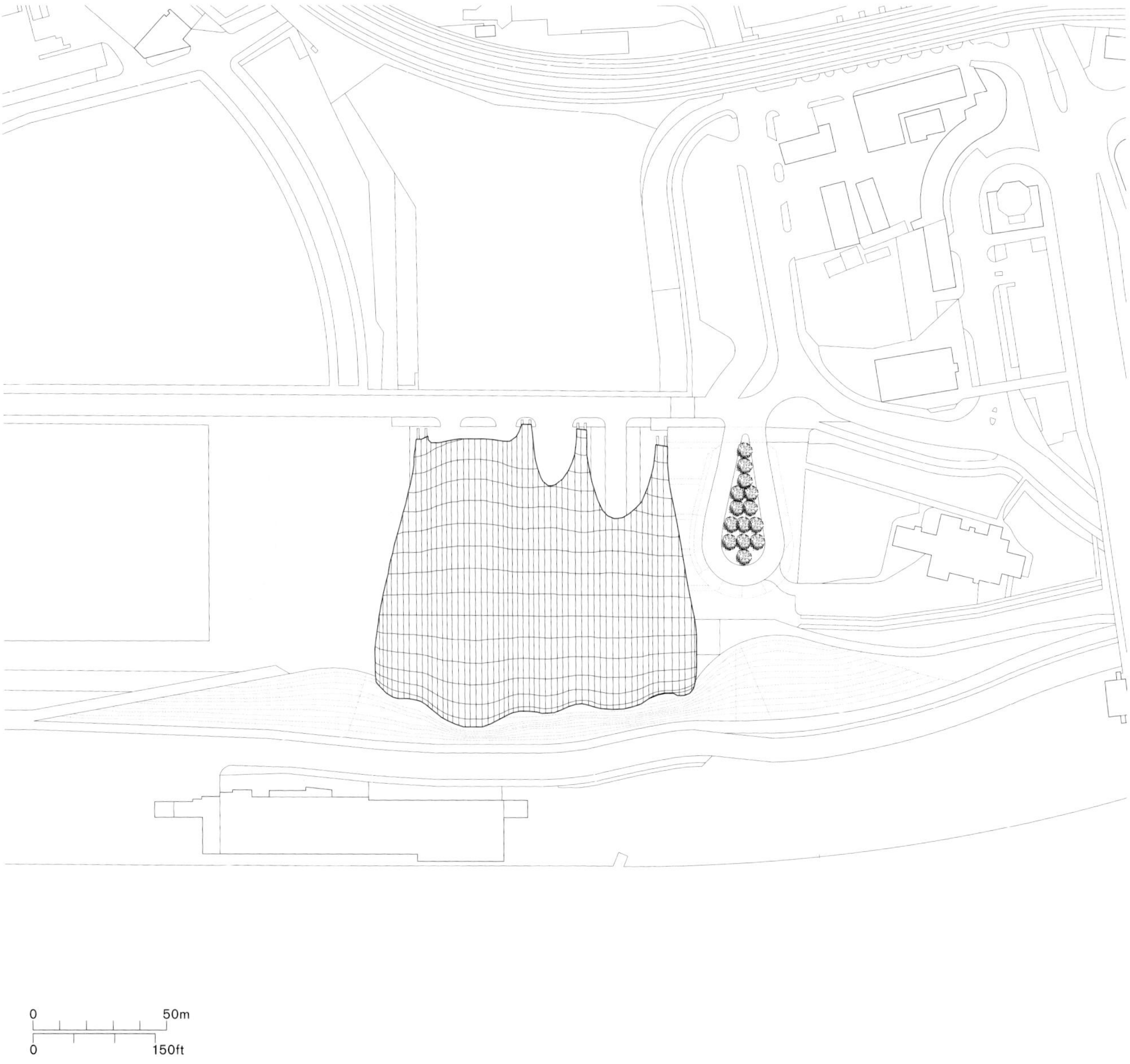

0 ———— 50m

0 ———— 150ft

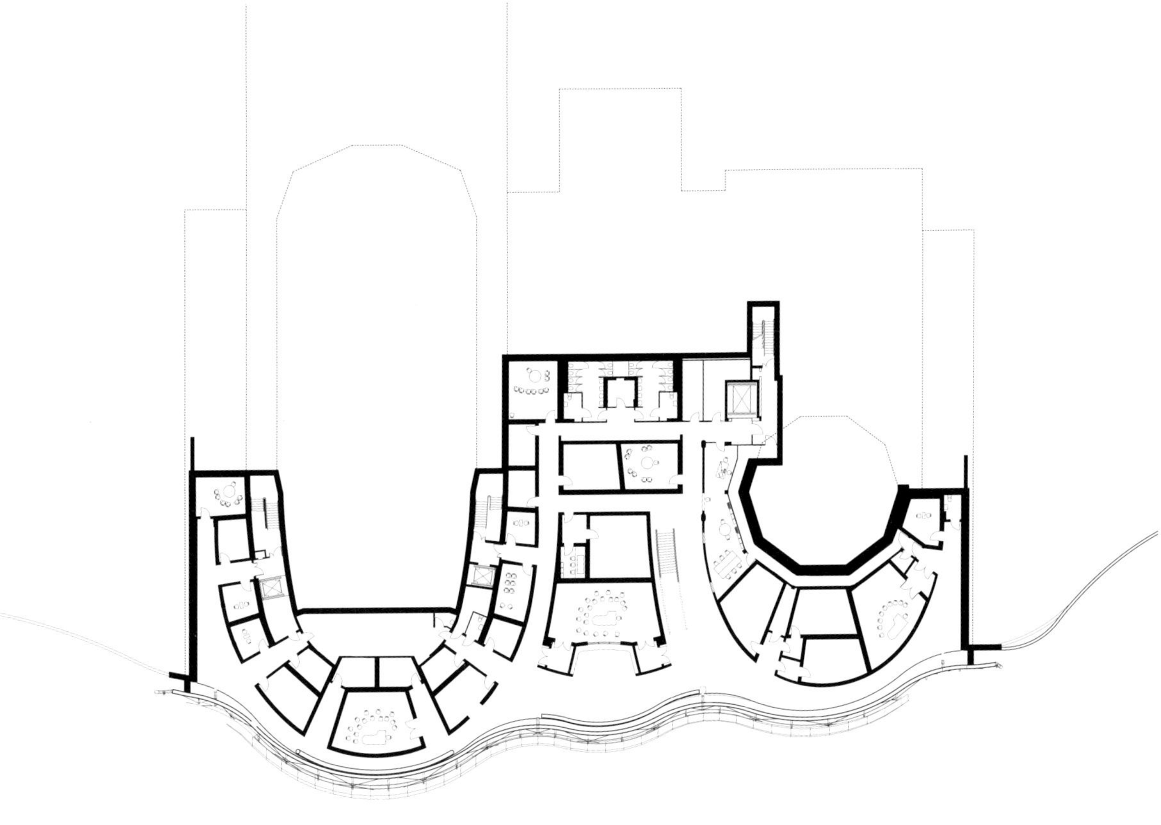

Left: A site plan showing the
fluid form of the building's roof.

Above: Plan at Music Education
Centre level, the lowest public
level in the building.

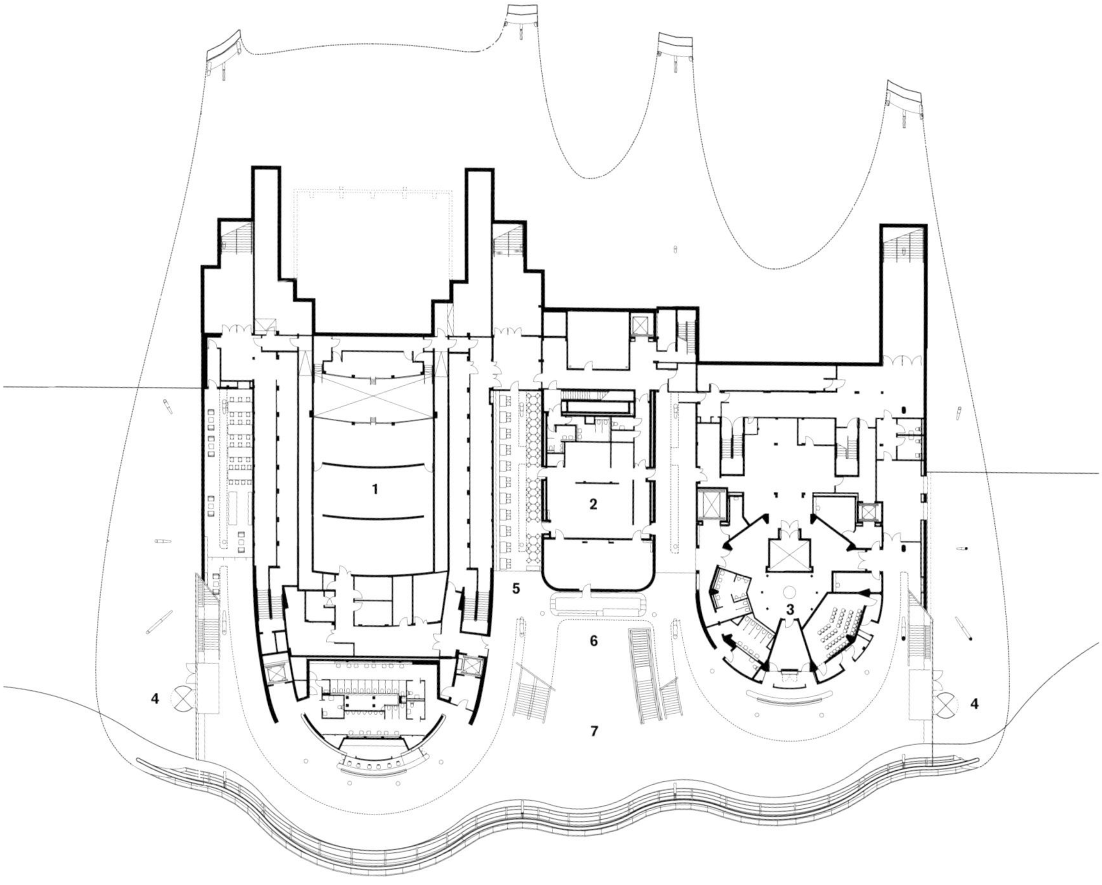

1

2

3

4

4

5

6

7

Above: Plan at Concourse
level, the principal public floor.

Right: Plan at stalls level.

0   20m

0   60ft

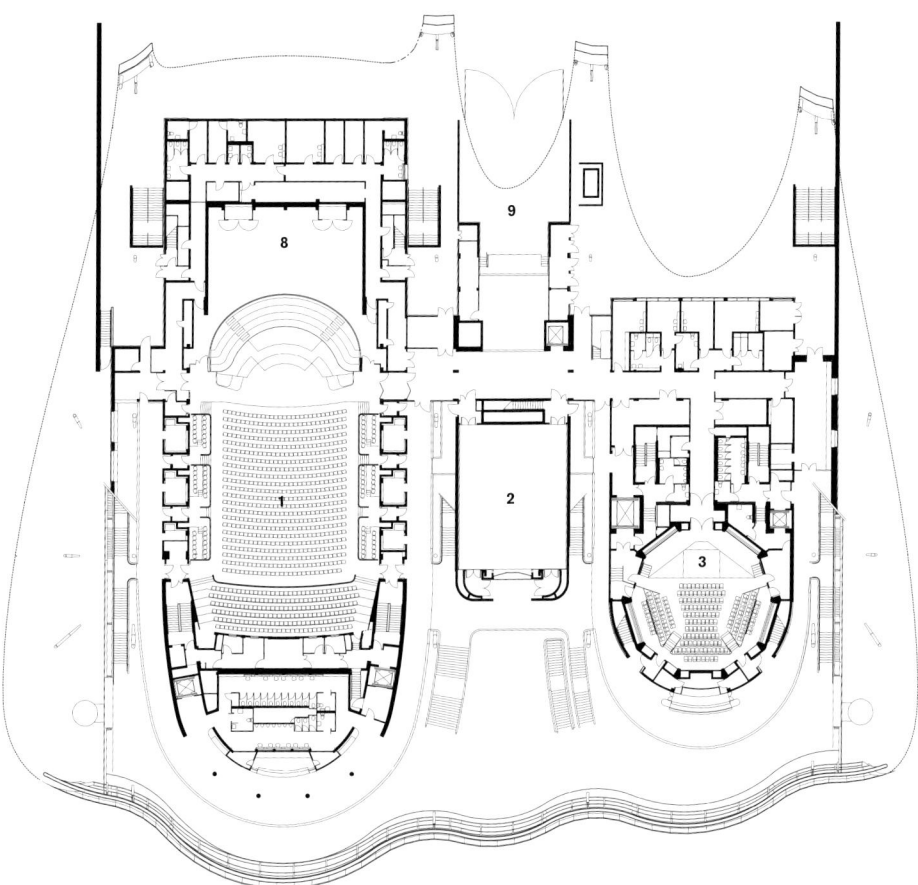

1 Hall One
2 Northern Rock Foundation Hall
3 Hall Two
4 public entrance
5 bar
6 Sir Michael Straker Café
7 Concourse
8 stage
9 loading bay

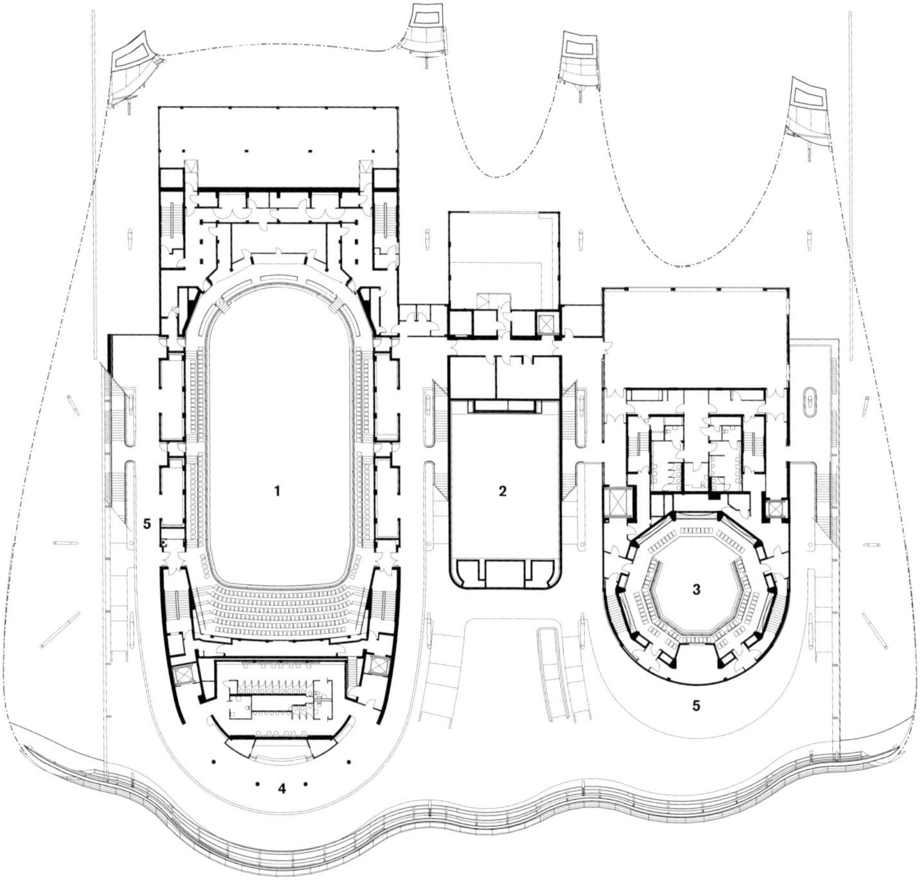

Above: Plan at tier 1 level.

Right: Plan at tier 2 level.

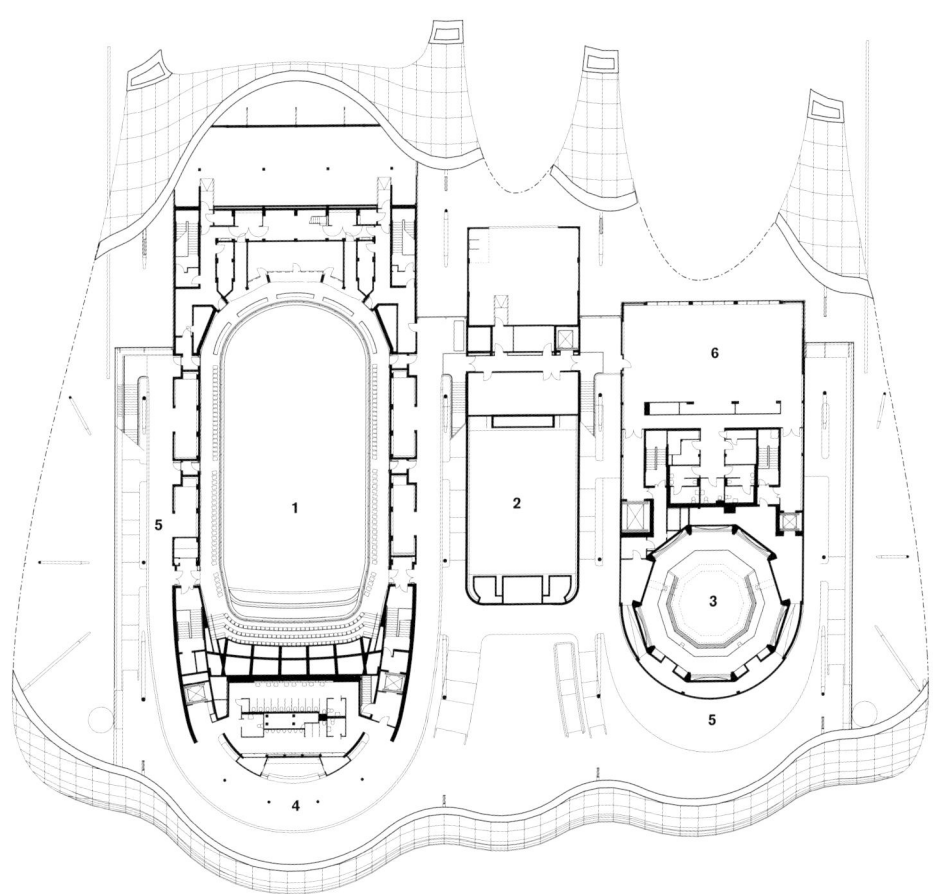

1 Hall One
2 Northern Rock Foundation Hall
3 Hall Two
4 bar
5 upper foyer
6 Barbour Room

A cross-section through the
1,700-seat Hall One, the
rehearsal space of the central
Northern Rock Foundation
Hall and the 450-seat Hall Two.
Below the floor of the Concourse
are loading and storage areas for
the halls; the Music Education
Centre occupies the lowest level.

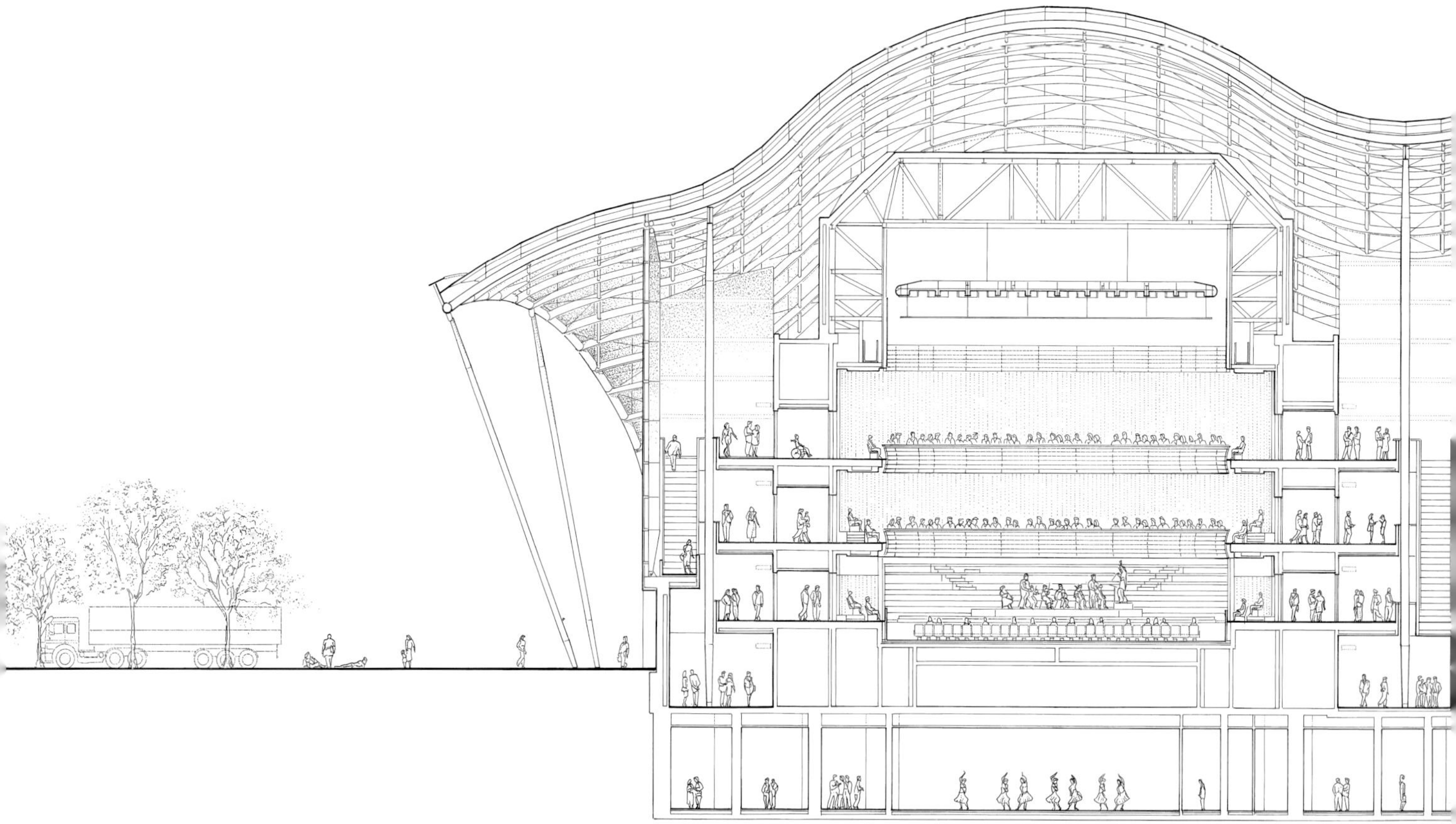

0   10m

0   30ft

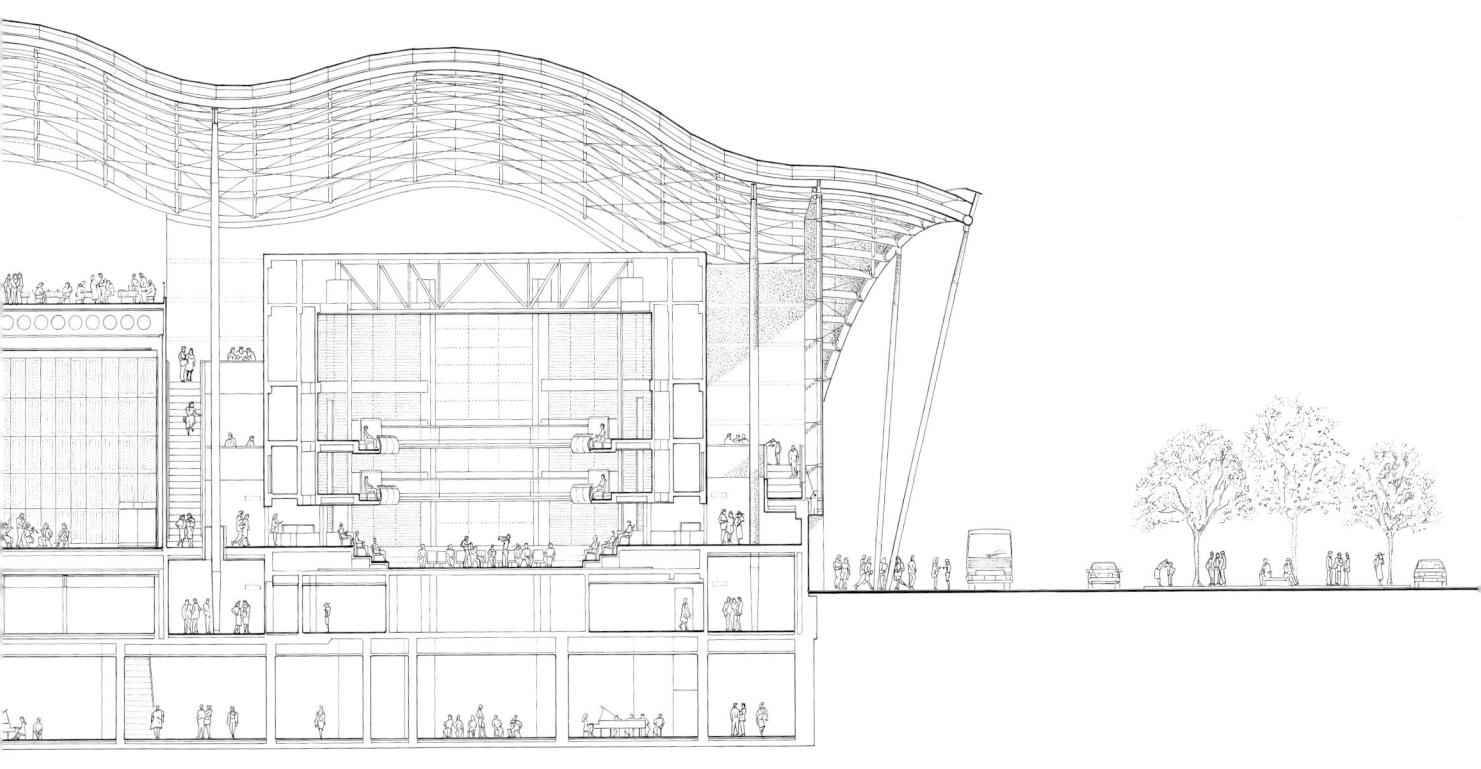

Left: The Sage Gateshead
glimpsed beneath the great
arch of the Tyne Bridge.

Above: Seen from a vantage
point on the Tyne Bridge,
The Sage Gateshead commands
the riverside. In the background
is the slender arc of the
Gateshead Millennium Bridge;
to the right of the bridge is the
Baltic Centre for Contemporary
Art, which occupies a converted
grain warehouse.

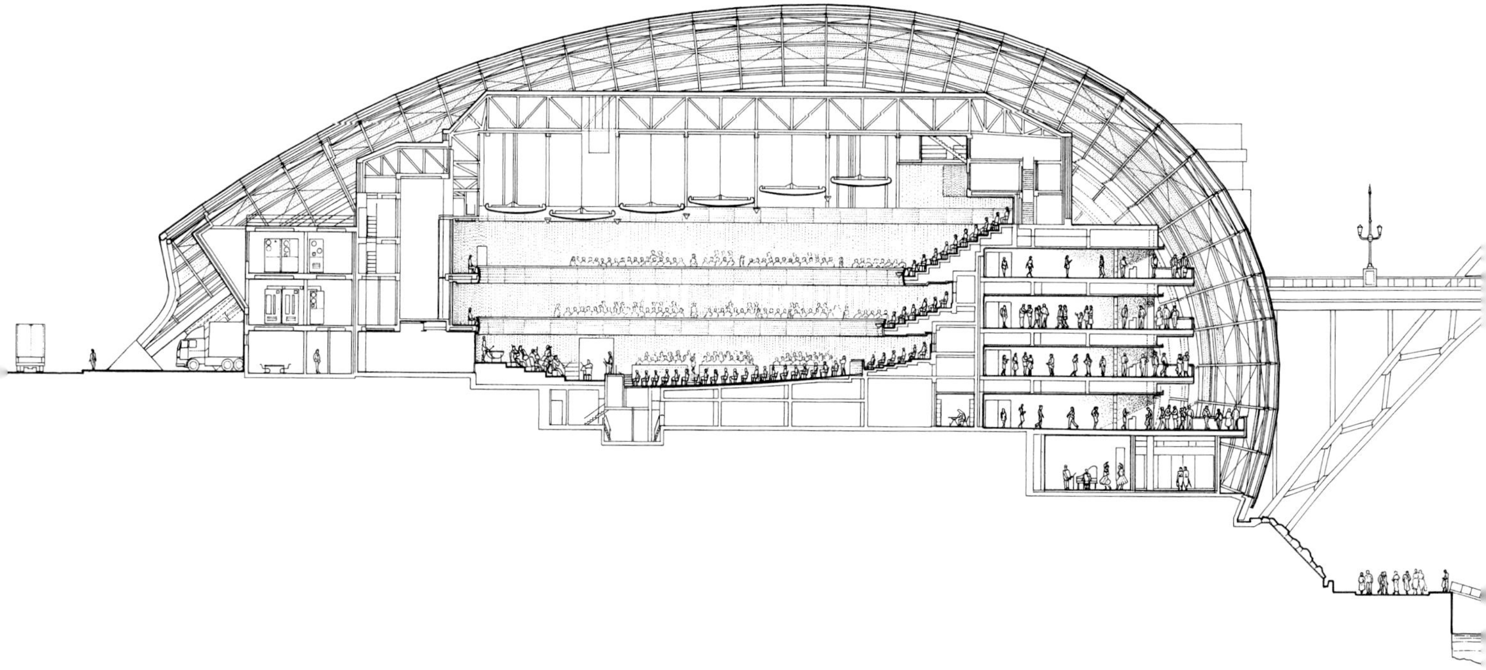

A cross-section through Hall
One, the largest of the three
auditoria, looking west towards
the Tyne Bridge.

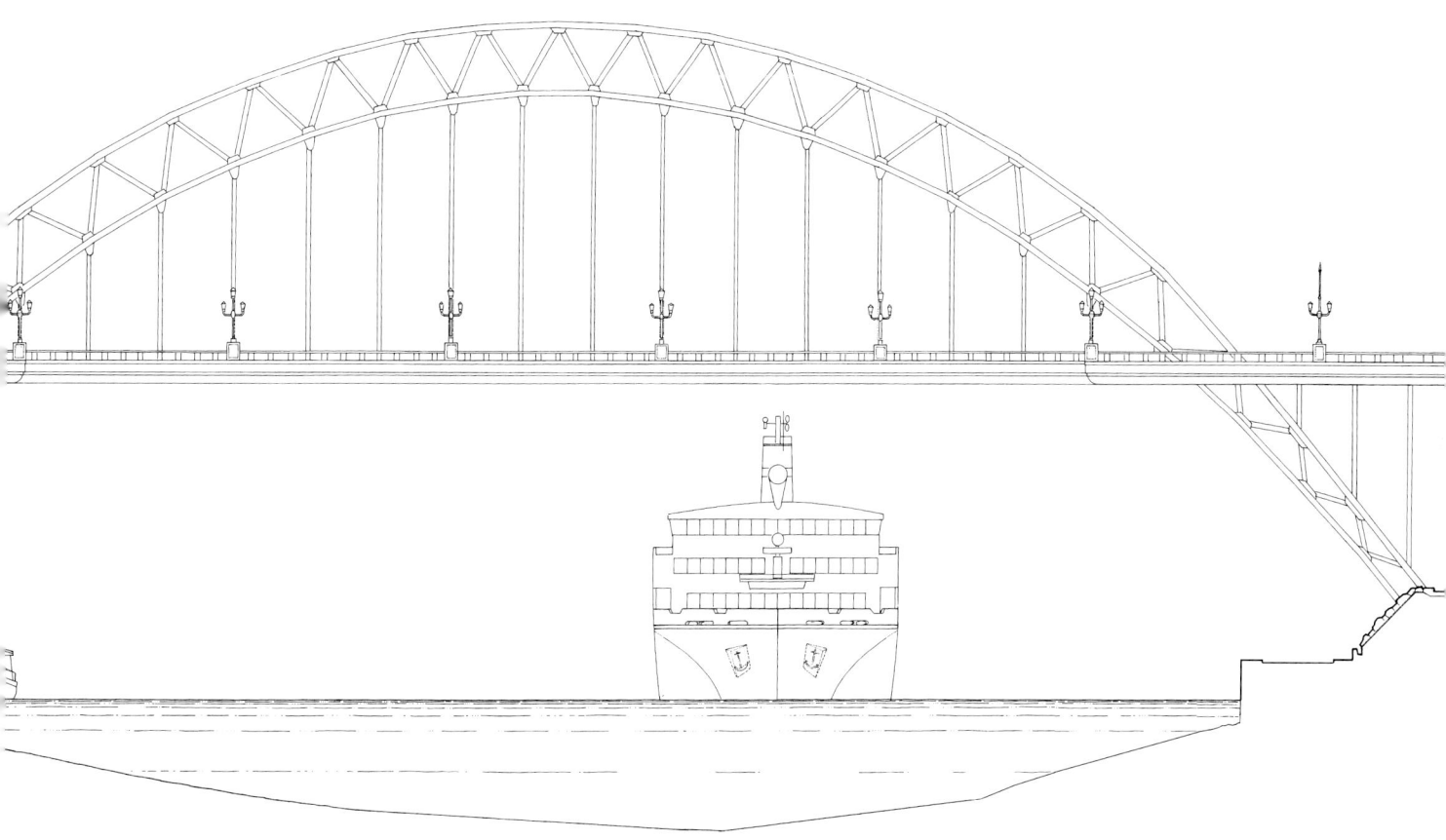

51

Above left: The building is serviced from the south; backstage servicing is clearly organised and efficient, with stages, loading docks and connecting routes all at the same level.

Above right: The taut form of the roof canopy and the building's affinity with the engineering traditions of Tyneside are evident in the springing points of the roof structure.

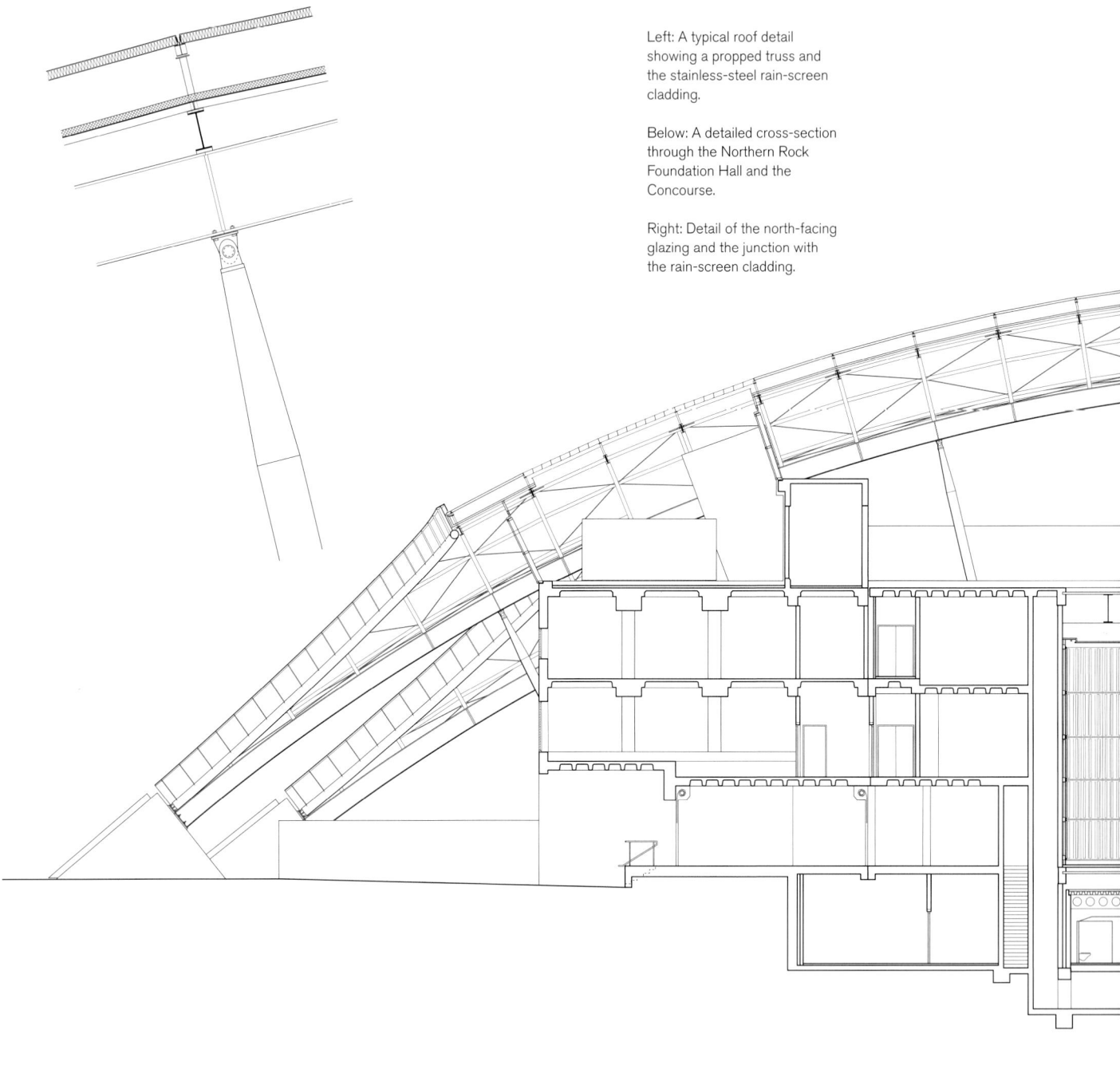

Left: A typical roof detail showing a propped truss and the stainless-steel rain-screen cladding.

Below: A detailed cross-section through the Northern Rock Foundation Hall and the Concourse.

Right: Detail of the north-facing glazing and the junction with the rain-screen cladding.

0   5m

0   15ft

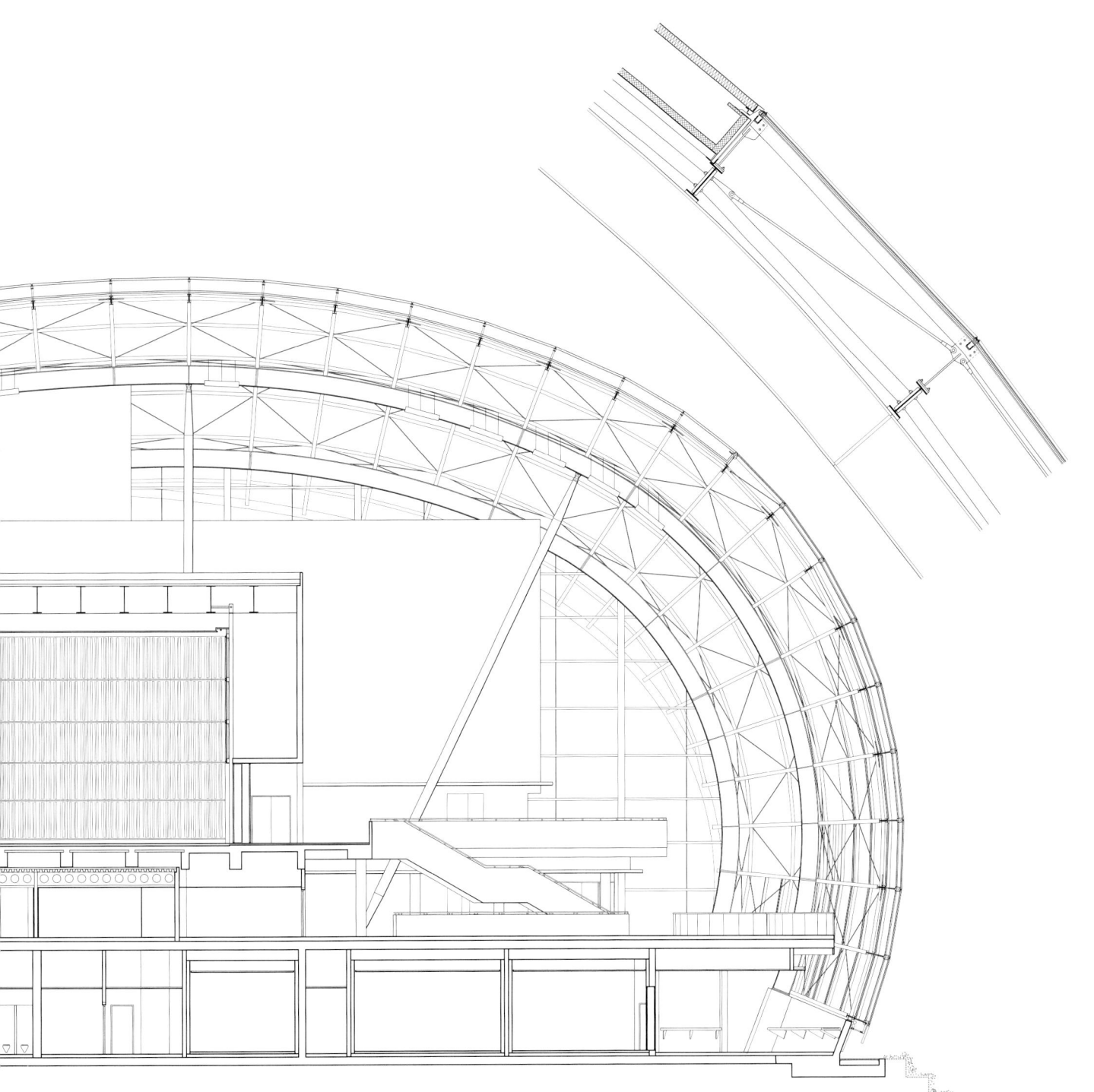

Above: The silvery roof is
mercurial, taking on different
moods and colour casts,
according to the changing
light and weather.

This is a building designed from first principles. Performance, acoustics, musicians and audiences are the keys to the design. The roof emerged as a kind of necessary umbrella to cover the auditoria, and was shaped to fit accordingly. Spencer de Grey, quoted in *The Guardian*, 26 November 2004

Above: Smooth and sensuous on the outside, on the inside the roof reveals its supporting framework with an industrial frankness.

We asked ourselves 'what is the nature of a performing arts centre in the twenty-first century?' We concluded that it should be open and inviting – not a temple to high culture.
Spencer de Grey, of Foster + Partners, in conversation with the editor, 2009

Above and right: The glazing that lines the waterfront steps up to allow views out from the Concourse, even from the highest gallery levels.

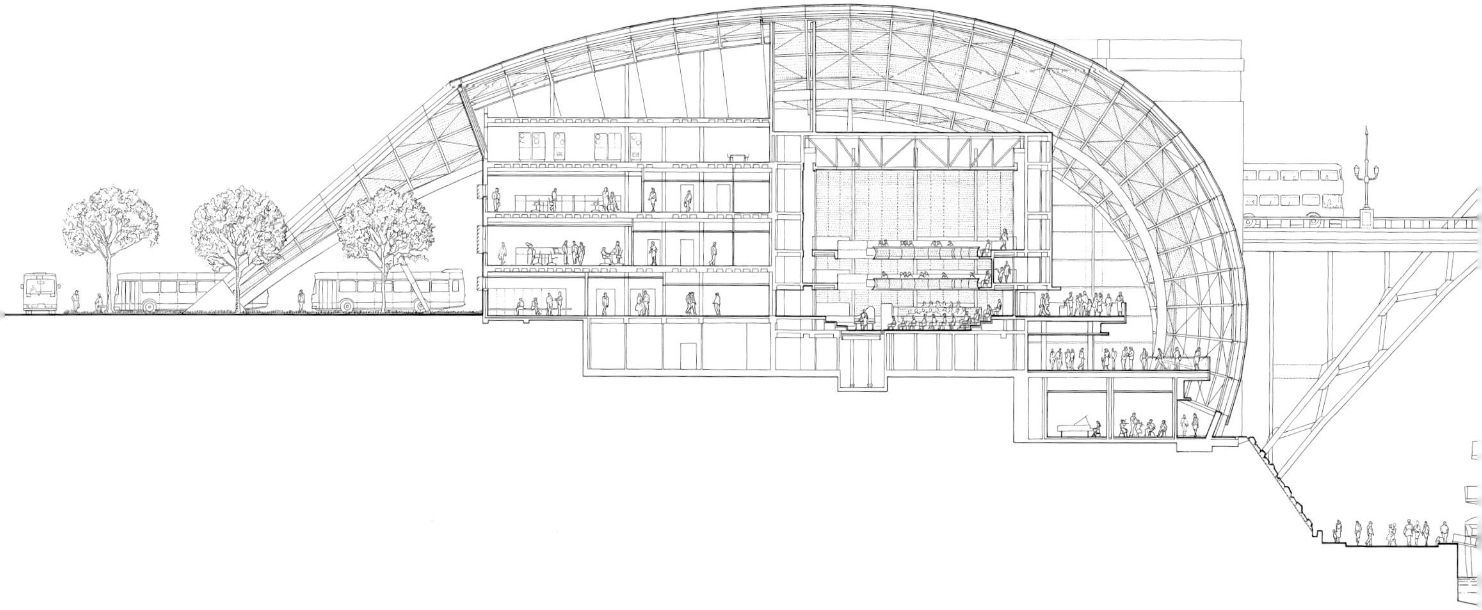

A north-south cross-section
through Hall Two, the backstage changing rooms and
administrative offices, looking
towards the Tyne Bridge.

0   10m

0   30ft

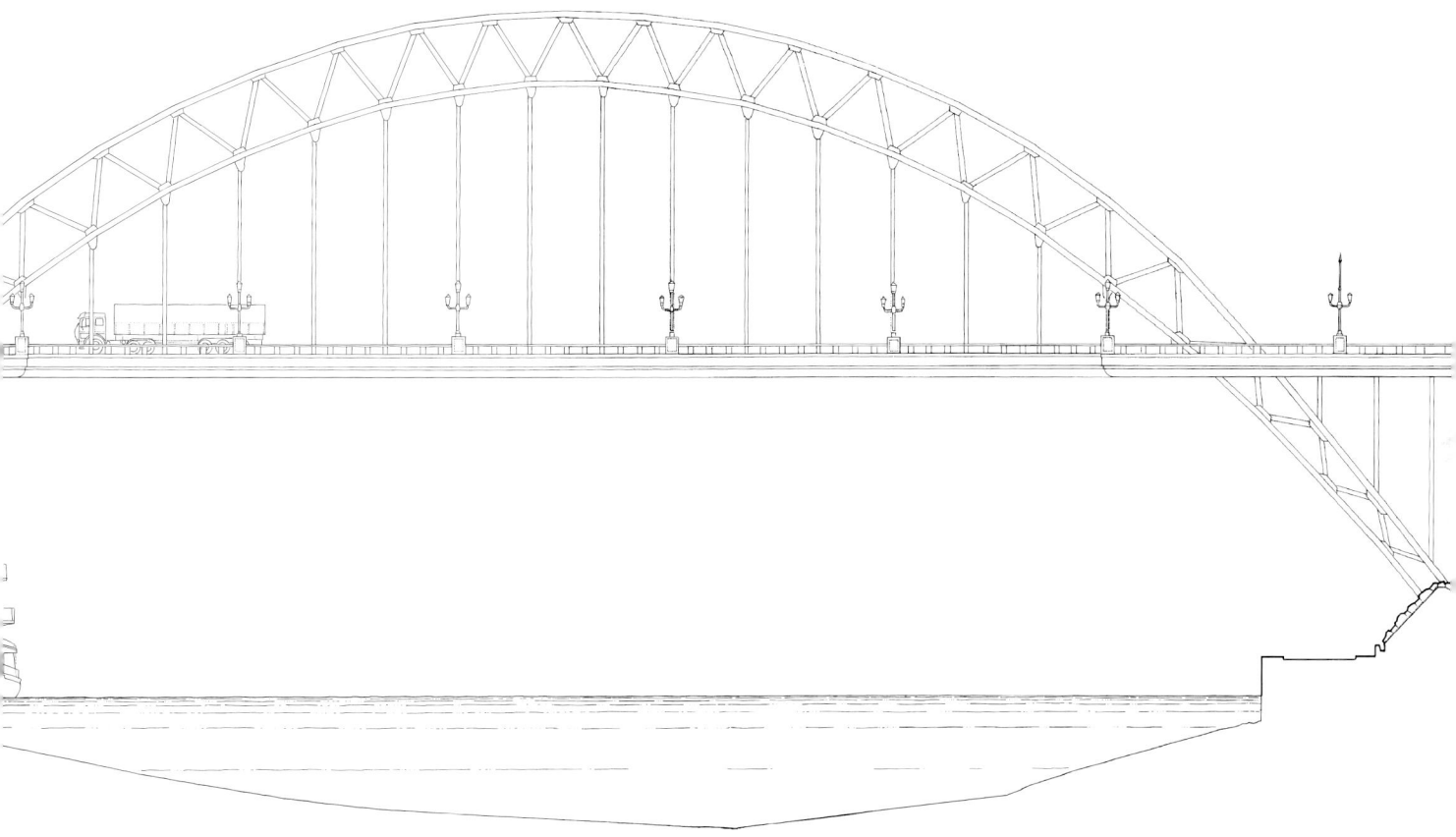

Previous pages: Looking out from the Concourse – the arch of the Tyne Bridge is framed by the arc of the roof.

Northern Rock
Foundation Hall

The Sir Michael Straker Café

Hal

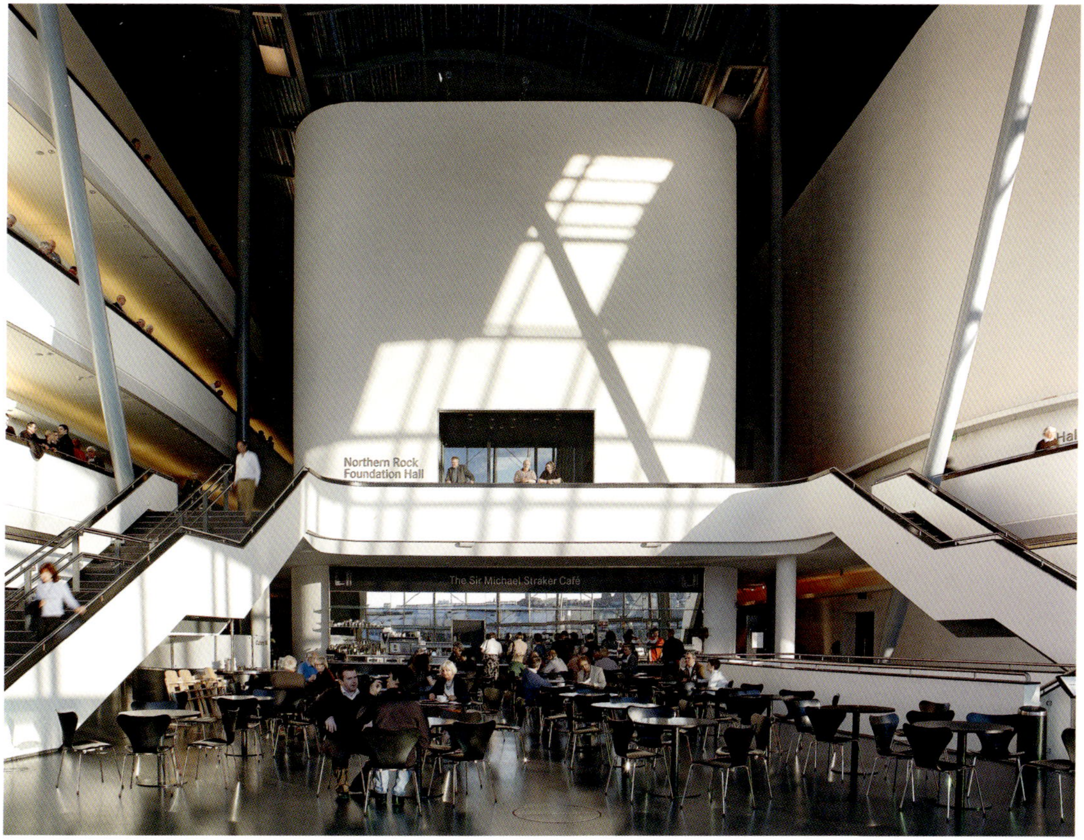

Within the Concourse, diverse
functions are combined within
a single enclosure, allowing
interaction between performers,
students and the public, and
breaking down cultural and
creative barriers. An atmosphere
of informality was encouraged
by limiting back-of-house green
rooms so that artists tend to
mix with their audiences.

The Concourse shelters a
major pedestrian route between
the Swing and Gateshead
Millennium Bridges, which means
that it is animated throughout the
day. When there are concerts, the
space encourages a wonderful
interaction between the
performers and the audience.

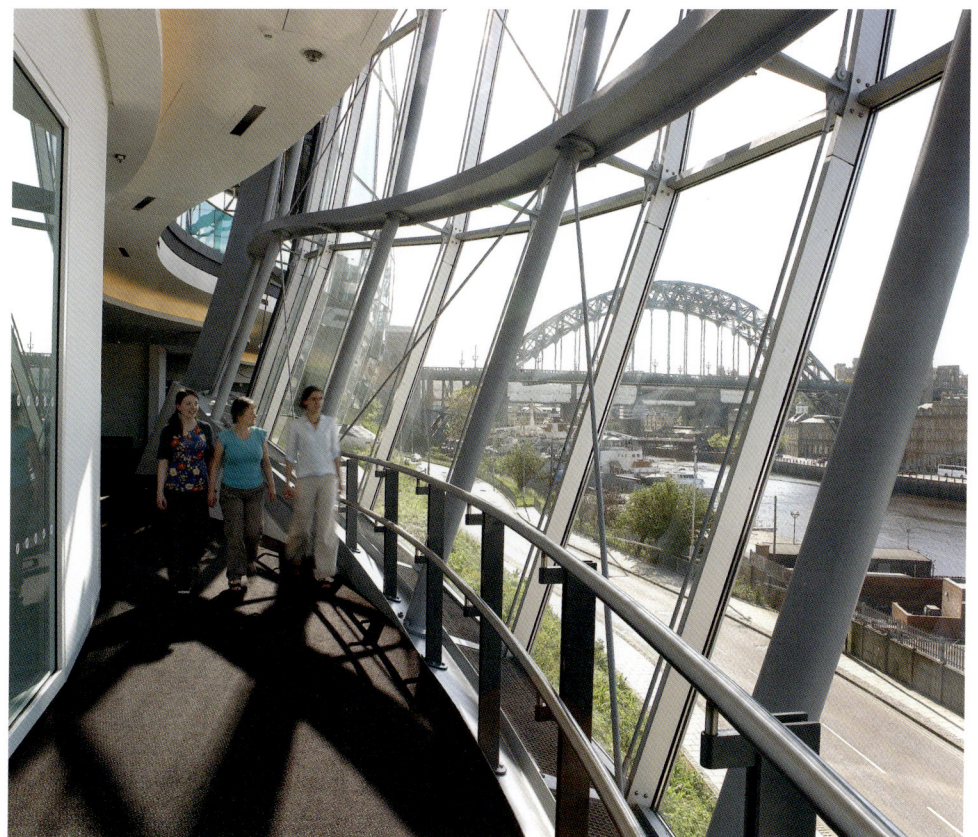

Left: The 100-metre-long glass
balustrade that runs through the
building was designed by glass
artist Kate Maestri. It adds a flash
of colour to the Concourse and
by piercing the building envelope
it reinforces the public route
through the space.

Above: The twenty-six rooms of
the Music Education Centre are
linked by a winding route that
looks out across the Tyne. By
exploiting the dramatic slope of
the site, it was possible to place
the Music Education Centre
beneath the Concourse, but to
maintain visual and acoustic
connections between the two.

Young musicians rehearse in the Northern Rock Foundation Hall; members of the public are invited to participate in these sessions whenever possible, either by sitting in or by observing through the large window that looks out on to the Concourse.

Northern Sinfonia, orchestra of
The Sage Gateshead, rehearse
on the stage of Hall One; the
stage can be adjusted to suit the
size of any orchestra or group by
adding or subtracting platforms
of various sizes and shapes.

Hall One is a derivative of the classic 'shoebox' concert hall. All the surfaces in the hall, including the balcony fronts, ceilings and even the seats, are profiled to help promote sound diffusion. The colour palette is a golden yellow, as distinct from the dark blue and deep red of the other two halls.

Overleaf: People gather in Hall One in readiness for a concert performance.

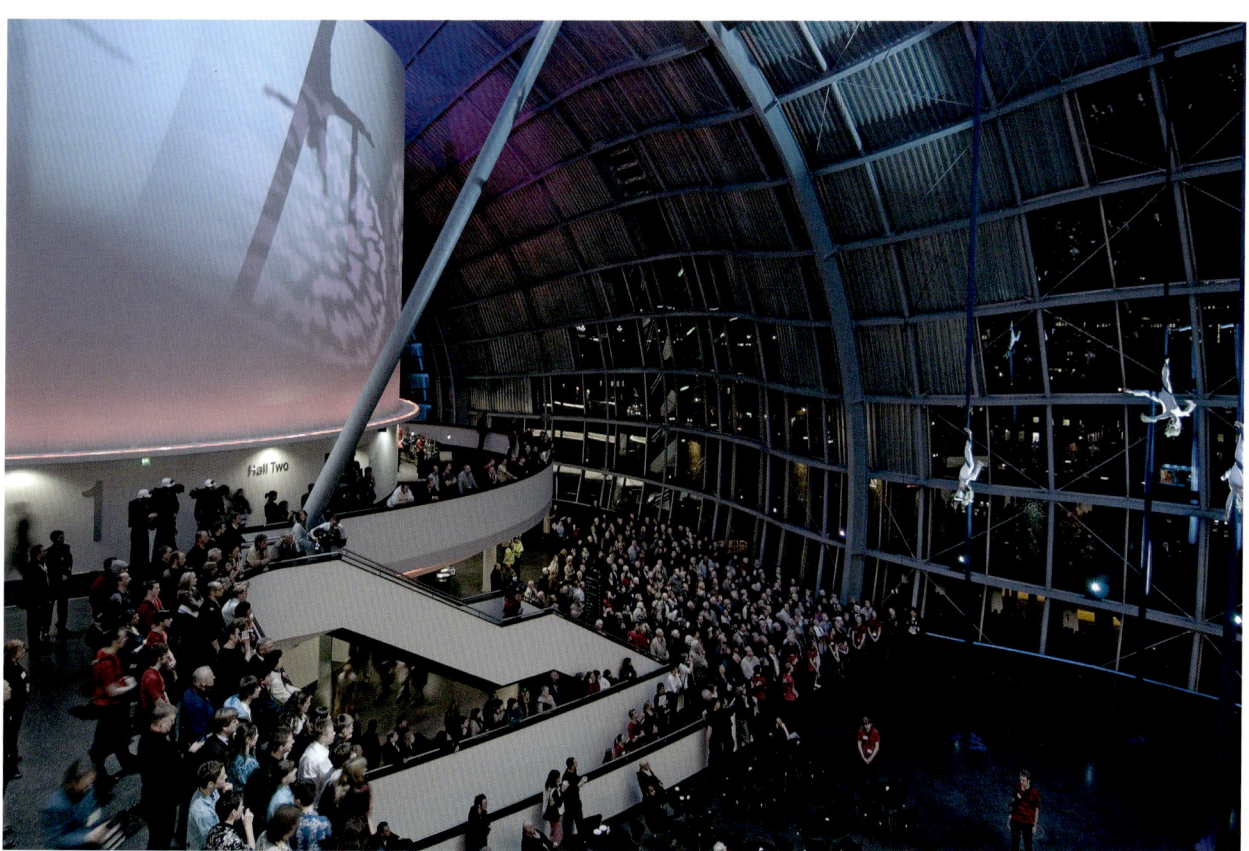

The Concourse is a space of almost infinite moods and possibilities, capable of being a performance venue in its own right when occasion demands. Dramatic lighting lends it a circus atmosphere, the roof evoking a big top.

The feel of the auditoria themselves is wonderful. The cool light wood casket of the main concert hall contrasts totally with the bohemian red of the small 'in the round' space – perfect for moody jazz. Peter Buchan, *Architecture Today*, March 2005

The 450-seat Hall Two is an intimate chamber room lined in deep red panelling. Its ten-sided plan, combined with reverberant wall surfaces and acoustic panels, 'spreads' the sound throughout the space, enveloping the audience in music.

Hall Two can accommodate a
variety of musical genres – from
chamber music to hip-hop, folk
and jazz. It has unobstructed
sight-lines and is planned to
encourage a strong sense of
interaction between performers
and audience.

Facts and figures

The Sage Gateshead
Gateshead, England
1997 – 2004
Client
  Gateshead Council
Project Team
  Simon Bowden
  Armin Buchbinder
  Murdoch Cameron
  Spencer de Grey
  Iain Fairbairn
  Jason Flanagan
  Norman Foster
  Daniel Goldberg
  Michael Gould
  Robert Harrison
  Karen Lambert
  Stuart Macalister
  Jason McColl
  Robin Partington
  Giada Pilo
  Austin Relton
  Katherine Ridley
  Paul Rogers
  Paul Simms
  Matthew Stokes
  George Stowell
Consultants
  Structural and Mechanical Engineer:
  Connell Mott MacDonald
  Specialist Engineers: Buro Happold
  (roof structure)
  Cost Consultants: Davis Langdon
  & Everest

Access Consultants: Burdus Access
Management
Planning Supervisor: WSP
Communications Design: Arup
Communications
Urban Movement Analysis: Space
Syntax Laboratories
Landscape Architect:
Desvigne & Dalnoky
Lighting Consultants: Equation
Lighting Design Ltd
Acoustic Engineers: Arup Acoustics
(Bob Essert)
Lift Consultants: Lerch Bates
Fire Consultants: Arup Fire
Theatre Consultants: Theatre
Projects Consultants
Catering Consultants:
Winton Nightingale
Main Contractor: Laing
O'Rourke Ltd
Specialist Roof Contractor:
Waagner Biro
Architectural Glass Artist:
Kate Maestri
Principal Awards
  2004 ICE North Robert Stephenson
  Award for Concept and Design
  2005 Retail & Leisure Property
  Award
  2005 RIBA Award
  2006 Civic Trust Award

Project chronology
1958 Northern Sinfonia founded
  by Michael Hall
1988 Folkworks established by Ros
  Rigby OBE and Alistair Anderson
1990 Northern Arts Strategic Review
  highlights the need for
  a regional music centre
1994 Feasibility study confirms viability
  of a regional music centre
1996 Gateshead Council wins
  competition to site new music
  centre
1997 Foster + Partners and Arup
  Acoustics win design competition
1999 First member of staff appointed
2000 Site clearance work completed
2001 Work begins on the building
  contract
2002 Sponsorship arrangements
  announced between The Sage
  Group plc, North Music Trust and
  Gateshead Council and the
  centre unveiled its permanent
  name and identity; since 5 July
  2002 the building has been
  known as The Sage Gateshead
2004 The last roof panel secured
  in place on 19 April 2004
2004 The Sage Gateshead opened to
  the public on 17 December 2004
2005 Royal opening by Her Majesty
  the Queen on 14 October 2005

2009 The Sage Gateshead celebrates its Fifth Birthday with a weekend of special events including workshops and performances by Kathryn Tickell with special guest Sting, Spiritualized, Northern Sinfonia, Andy Sheppard and The Zehetmair Quartet

Performance spaces

Hall One

A 'shoebox'-shaped hall with seating for up to 1,700 people on one, two or three levels. The hall has been designed to the highest international standards and acoustically specified to maximise audience enjoyment for all types of music. A dance/orchestra pit is an added option to the space.

Hall Two

This flexible space for up to 400 is believed to be the first ten-sided performing arts space in the world. Audiences can be placed seated or standing, on three levels, and it is also designed to the highest international standards and acoustically specified for both acoustic and amplified music.

Northern Rock Foundation Hall

The acoustic in this space mirrors that of Hall One to allow smooth transfer from rehearsal to performance. The Hall features a large window to the Concourse allowing the public to watch rehearsals and the musicians to play in an environment lit with natural light. The hall is also used for performances, workshops, weddings, dinners and conference events.

Music Education Centre

Comprises twenty-six rooms dedicated to music education and community music with spaces for teaching, practice, workshops and recording.

Barbour Room

A dedicated entertainment suite, catering for up to 300 people.

Funding

Building Cost
    £70 million
Building Funding
    Arts Council England
    European Regional Development
    Fund
    One North East
Founding Patrons
    The Sage Group plc
    The Barbour Trust
    Northern Rock Foundation
    The Garfield Weston Foundation
    Joan and Margaret Halbert
Endowment Donors
    The Shears Foundation
    Mrs Cynthia Goldman and
    the Goldman Family
    The Go-Ahead Group
    Northern Arts Board
    Benfield Charitable Trust
    1989 Willan Trust
    The David Boardman Trust
    Roland Cookson Fund
    Fenwick Ltd
    Northumbrian Water
    Sir James Knott Trust

Building structure

The gross building area is 20,000 square metres; total building enclosure area is 12,000 square metres

The curved steel roof structure weighs 750 tonnes

The cladding comprises 3,000 stainless steel panels and 250 glazed panels; laid flat, the roof covers 12,000 square metres – big enough to accommodate two football pitches

The stainless-steel roof panels vary in length between 2 and 4 metres and are 1 metre wide; the average weight is 80 kg; the largest glazed panels measure 4 × 2 metres and weigh 300 kg

More than 18,000 cubic metres of concrete was used in the foundations and the halls – enough to fill twenty-three competition-size swimming pools

More than 1,100 concrete and steel piles were sunk into the ground to support the massive structure

Most of the 3,858 tonnes of steel used forms reinforcement in the foundations and the walls and floors

At its highest point The Sage Gateshead is 40 metres high, twice the height of the Angel of the North

The coloured glass Concourse balustrade is 100 metres long and was created by architectural glass artist Kate Maestri

Key facts

The Sage Gateshead is the permanent home of Northern Sinfonia, Music Director Thomas Zehetmair, and Folkworks, Artistic Director, Kathryn Tickell. Both are integrated into the management structure of the charitable company responsible for the building and its programme

Over 400 performances and 38,000 learning and participation sessions take place every year in the building. The Sage Gateshead has become a regional icon, resource and, along with the other cultural infrastructure in the region, a driver of economic prosperity, a magnet for its communities, for business and for tourism

Northern Sinfonia, Folkworks, Gateshead Council and Northern Arts (now Arts Council England North East) were the four founding partners

The building is open sixteen hours a day, seven days a week, 362 days a year

During its opening year The Sage Gateshead hosted 438 performances and 12,319 Learning and Participation sessions and welcomed approximately 750,000 visitors

School visits to The Sage Gateshead are popular – since opening, thirty-seven Gateshead schools have visited, totalling almost 1,400 Gateshead school children

For every £1 invested in The Sage Gateshead by way of revenue funding in its first year, it returned a total of £11 into the regional economy

The Sage Gateshead created over 400 new jobs

In May 2006, The Sage Gateshead hosted BBC Young Musician of the Year. Over one million viewers saw the Final on BBC2: the equivalent of a full house in Hall One every night for almost twenty months

Credits

Editor: David Jenkins
Design: Thomas Manss
& Company; Thomas Manss,
Enrica Corzani, Keira Yang
Picture Research:
Kathryn Tollervey
Proofreading: Julia Dawson
Production Supervision:
Martin Lee
Reproduction: DawkinsColour
Printed and bound in Italy
by Grafiche SiZ S.p.A.

The FSC-certified paper
gardamatt has been supplied
by Cartiere del Garda S.p.A., Italy

Picture Credits

Photographs
© Richard Bryant/Arcaid: 72,
88 – 89
Foster + Partners: 14
© Peter Cook/VIEW: 66 – 67, 80
© Graeme Peacock: 6 – 7
Nigel Young: Front cover, 16, 18,
20, 22, 24, 25, 28, 29, 30, 31,
32, 33, 34 – 35, 42 – 43, 46 – 47,
48, 49, 52, 53, 54 – 55, 58, 59,
60, 61, 62 – 63, 68, 69, 70, 71,
73, 74 – 75, 76 – 77, 78 – 79, 81,
82 – 83, 84, 85, 86, 87, 94 – 95

Drawings and Sketches
Birds Portchmouth Russum:
44 – 45, 50 – 51, 64 – 65
Foster + Partners: 19, 23, 26, 27,
56 – 57
Norman Foster: 4 – 5, 15
Gregory Gibbon: 12 – 13
John Hewitt: 18, 20, 21
William McElhinney: 36, 37, 38,
39, 40, 41

Every effort has been made
to contact copyright holders.
The publishers apologise for
any omissions which they will
be pleased to rectify at the
earliest opportunity.

Editor's Note

In editing this book I am
particularly grateful to Anthony
Sargent and Peter Buchanan for
their invaluable contributions. I
would also like to thank Thomas
Manss, Enrica Corzani and Keira
Yang for bringing the book to life
graphically; Kathryn Tollervey,
who mined the office archive;
Julia Dawson for proofreading
the text; Martin Lee for
coordinating production; and the
numerous people in the Foster
studio – past and present –
who helped piece together the
background to the project. I
would like to express special
thanks to Helen Larmouth and
Helen Fussell at The Sage
Gateshead for helping to move
the project along smoothly
behind the scenes.

David Jenkins
London, May 2010